PLACE␂

POWER & ENERGY

*At last, a book that answers the questions about
the Sedona vortexes and the mystery behind them*

"This book takes us on a fascinating journey with a good friend.
We are grateful that Worrell shares his artistic creativity and
writings not only in our gallery but also with us personally."
DIANE & MARTY HERMAN, *Exposures Gallery, Sedona*

"Bill Worrell views the world differently than most because he has spent
a lifetime exercising his intuitive eye. There is no one better to take the
reader to places of Mystery, Power and Energy than Worrell."
ROBERT TITLEY, *Nashville Music Manager*

"If we are good witnesses, we can see the world through Worrell's
magic with words. But this book also gives us a glimpse into the heart,
mind, and soul of a great artist."
KIX BROOKS, *Nashville songwriter-performer*

"Association with places of power has influenced Worrell's art: rock art
sites, deserts, canyon lands, rivers, ancient forests, and mountain tops.
His stories salute many of these places of power."
WYMAN MEINZER, *author-photographer*

"The stories collected here could be enhanced only by listening
to Worrell telling them around a riverside campfire."
JUDY SKEEN, PH.D, *Belmont University*

"Bill Worrell has been my inspirational source of mystery,
power, and energy since I was six years old."
JAY BOY ADAMS, *Worrell Gallery, Santa Fe*

"The privilege of representing Bill Worrell's work to the public has been a
powerful experience. I witness evidence of mystery, power and the energy
that flows from within Bill on a daily basis."
MARY ADAMS, *Worrell Gallery, Santa Fe*

PLACES OF MYSTERY, POWER & ENERGY

OTHER BOOKS BY
BILL WORRELL:

Colorado City, Texas (1977) A Photographic Essay

Voices From the Caves – The Shamans Speak
(First printing 1996, Second printing 1998)

Journeys Through the Winds of Time (2000)

FORTHCOMING:

Anthology – A Collection of Worrell's Thoughts, Songs,
Poems and Writings

Outside the Lines – A Journey Through the World of Art

El Coyote del Llano – A Collection of Coyote Stories

Eye of a Needle – A Treatise on Possessions
and Looking Back

Conversations with Ellie – Conversations Between
Worrell and His Dog, a Book of Satire about
Public Education, Organized Religion, Organized
Politics (an oxymoron), and Metaphysical Notions
by Bill Worrell
& Ellie May Lucille Worrell

Worrell

PLACES OF MYSTERY, POWER & ENERGY

A Nonfictional Anthology

by Bill Worrell

IRIE
BOOKS

Places of Mystery, Power and Energy is published by Irie Books,
Bokeelia, Florida.

Cover image: *Near Sedona, Arizona* by Bill Worrell
All other photographs and artwork in this book by Bill Worrell except
Mystery, Power & Energy by Marc Bennett, White Oak Studios,
Fredericksburg, Texas.
Capote Falls by Spider Johnson
Ancient Paintings on Cave Wall and *Tornado* by Wyman Meinzer
Drawing by Jim Eppler *(Hill Country Magic)*
The Cliffs of Step Mountain by Marti Perkins
Step Mountain from above by Spider Johnson
The Author in the Abandoned Chair by Gretchen Bataille

Cover and interior design: ital art by Mariah Fox
Body text set to Adobe Caslon Pro. Headings: Trade Gothic.

For information regarding gallery affiliations and other inquiries,
please contact
BillWorrell.com
8111 Lower Willow Creek Road
Mason, Texas 76856

ISBN 13: 978-1-62755-381-0
First Edition

10 9 8 7 6 5 4 3 2 1

ACKNOWLEDGMENTS

THIS BOOK would not be near what is before readers' eyes were it not for Ross Lewallen, longtime jeweler in Santa Fe. As the manuscript was about to be printed Ross intervened and introduced me to Gerry and Lorry Hausman, publishers, and thus to their daughter, Mariah Fox, university professor and book designer. The author owes more to these people than can be tacitly stated. Thanks is also given to Mary and Jay Adams, owners of the Worrell Gallery in Santa Fe, New Mexico; to Marty and Diane Herman and Exposures International Gallery of Fine Art in Sedona, Arizona; to Scott Haupert and Manny Silerio, owners of Sandstone Cellars, Mason, Texas; to Cory McBride and Winnifred Patton, owners of Zapotec Art, Houston, Texas; and to Karin Newby (former owner), Leroy Doyle, and Kim Roseman of the Karin Newby Gallery in Tubac, Arizona.

Were credit and mention given to all deserving people this book would be pages longer, and even then I would inadvertently leave some deserving person's name unmentioned. I am so grateful to all of you.

INDEX OF CHAPTERS

	Preface	1
	Author's Note	3
I	Space, Matter, and Energy	9
II	Compelling Evidence	13
III	Negative Energies	17
IV	Fort McKavett	19
V	Spiritual Energy	29
VI	Electronic Energy	31
VII	A Friend of Long Ago	35
VIII	A Ghostly Energy	41
IX	The Marfa Lights	43
X	The Lubbock Lights	47
XI	Fraternities	51
XII	Energy of an Artist	63
XIII	Energy From Good Advice	67
XIV	Giving and Receiving	71
XV	A Santa Fe Ambience	75
XVI	El Santuario de Chimayo	79
XVII	The Gallinas River	85
XVIII	The Lower Pecos River	93
XIX	The Tunnel of Light	101
XX	Invisible Forces	105
XXI	Keller's Store	119
XXII	Hill Country Magic	121
XXIII	A Casita	125
XXIV	Ravens Can Learn to Talk	133
XXV	The Monastery	137
XXVI	Ancient and Modern Energies	143
XXVII	The Orchid Gown	147
XXVIII	April Dance	153
XXIX	Magical Sedona	159

INDEX OF CHAPTERS

XXX	The Steel Trap	171
XXXI	The Winds of Fate	181
XXXII	Mitchell County, Texas	191
XXXIII	God and the Fallen Angel	199
XXXIV	Nipple Peak	207
XXXV	Step Mountain	213
XXXVI	Hell's Gate	219
XXXVII	Old Time Religion	225
XXXVIII	Lost and Found	235
XXXIX	The Energies of Personalities	241
XL	The Eagle Nest Lodge	245
XLI	Divining	253
	Epilogue	257
	A Parting Note	259
	Bill Worrell Biography	261

PREFACE

BILL WORRELL'S personal journal begins with phrases that ring true—"I came from the desert, from the dust of the desert." And he rounds it out with – "I must return again and again to the desert that gave me life."

Worrell does not say this lightly. He means it literally, as in wandering man. And spiritually, as in wandering soul. For he is both. And whether he is talking about the mystery of the Lubbock Lights with which he had two encounters in his life, or just writing about the abundant Hill Country magic around his Texas ranch, he is always at home talking about the things he loves: his dog Ellie May Lucille, his family, his friends.

He gives good advice (one of the chapters in the book) and who better to do so than a professor-sculptor-painter-writer-philosopher. Truthfully, Worrell is in a category all by himself–silver-tongued, biblically graced, and so well-minded in the old sense of the word that one thinks of Aristotle on the Panhandle picking up shards from our earliest beginnings and fitting them into the present moment.

The book you hold in your hands may be a personal journal but it moves like the man himself. Or as we might say, the spirit of Man himself. For it is a book of universal self-examination. It is the story of our origins on the mythic sands of time. And as much as anything else, it tells us that all things live, are alive, and are indivisible. This is the mind of the mystic who sees the numberless stars of a clear night and is transported far across the desert horizon on his own imagination, horseman to the stars, dreamer, maker of worlds, whorls, whirls, Worrells.

– *GERALD HAUSMAN*

AUTHOR'S NOTE

I CAME FROM THE DESERT, from the dust of the desert. To the desert I must return to someday again be that dust of the desert from whence I came. I will fulfill the scriptures and return again to the desert dust, to those sands that shift with the winds endlessly, forever blowing across and among the earth's many transfixing wonders. Ah, but until then I am flesh, and as such I will and I must return again and again to the desert that gave me life. I am compelled, constantly compelled, to return to it to visit, to muse, to marvel, to meditate, to absorb its wonderful and enlightening energies, and to stand in its presence in awe. Just to be there, as it might be said; I must be there just to be there.

My desert emergence occurred in El Paso, Texas, in 1935. Not long afterward, I was transplanted to Colorado City, Texas, which is also a desert. It is a place in the Permian Basin. In the time between El Paso and Colorado City, there was a very short—less than a two-year stay—in Seagraves, Texas. Seagraves is another desert habitat, one where early settlers plowed and sowed seeds in fields of sand, always praying for rain, always hoping for some bumper crop, and almost always reaping less than meager harvests. It was a place my earthly father thought would boom and become what Lubbock, Texas, now is. That did not happen so we moved on. We moved to Colorado City—a less harsh, less windy, less sandy and dusty, and far less depressing place—yet still a place of the desert, but one that had many more ribbons of life than did the other places.

It did not take too many years for me to realize my bond with this intriguing landscape and to realize I had some obligation to it. I have been compelled to paint it, sculpt it, and to re-arrange minute parts of it into all sorts of creations. Then, for lack of a better word, or perhaps wistfulness of some sort, I call what I have done—what I have created, what I have re-arranged—"art."

Thus for all my mortal life I have been creating art, although I did not realize I had been doing this until our mother died. After this sad event, I was going through things in the family homestead, and to my amazement and delight, I found things I had sculpted, carved, and drawn when I was but a young child.

The discovery that I have "always been an artist" came well after I received recognition for such and became affiliated with various art galleries across the country, primarily galleries located in the Southwest. Because these galleries are located in desert states, I have been privileged to travel to and within their environs. I have driven hundreds of thousands of miles on their highways. I have driven thousands of miles on their back roads—those narrow, rough, and winding meanders that have led me to incredible vistas and unbelievably fascinating and mysterious adventures.

Sedona, Arizona is where the idea for this book germinated, but more fundamentally, the genesis goes back in time decades and decades to those days and places where in wanderlust I drove those desert back roads, camped beside streams, and sat around campfires while playing a Martin Guitar and writing songs. So although the idea came while in Sedona—as I pondered the fascination people have with the vortexes in and surrounding that village—it goes far beyond that one place, even extending into the energies of personalities. These are true writings and stories. They deal with not only other places in Arizona, but also with places in New Mexico, Colorado, and Texas. The vignettes range from natural phenomena to ghostly presences. There are accounts of such strange occurrences as the Lubbock Lights, apparitions, the Marfa Lights, UFOs, and of course, Vortexes.

This book is not a scientific or a scholarly exegesis. It is simply an anthology of a few (among many) of an artist's experiences and observations in various Southwestern places. It has been in thought and progress for several years. It is a compilation of various writings and stories from my journals. It is also a compilation of memories. Thoughts, memories, writings, and notes very often overlap, so there may be some overlapping and repetitious information in the stories. Publishing this book has not been a particularly easy process, and a book could be written about that subject. I am very grateful to the many friends and family members who have contributed ideas and advice to this publication.

If the reader does not read through to the end, it is unlikely he or she will get much from these writings, and for readers who do read to the end, there still might not be much for some of them to gain. It is my wish, however, that those who read these writings derive at least some entertainment from them, if nothing else. More than this, I hope readers gain a few important insights and come to a state of open-mindedness about happenings that seem to be metaphysical.

The only fiction contained herein is the changing of actual names. In some instances I did this to protect certain individuals from scorn or disdain or to preserve their privacy.

Love, Peace, Joy, Healing, Freedom, & LIGHT to you,

BILL WORRELL

MYSTERY, POWER, & ENERGY

There are places of Great Mystery
Great Power
Great Energy

Some of these are good
Some are not good

Watch closely every step taken
So that Mysteries edify you
Subsidize your faith
And not confound you

That the Power surrounding you
Be that goodness of the Great Spirit

And that the Energy be boundless
Endless
Joyful
And filled with Great Peace

POWERFUL VISTAS SURROUND SEDONA.

I.
SPACE, MATTER & ENERGY

SOME BELIEVE there is energy scattered throughout the universe—
that it is infinite. I am among those who believe this. I cannot imagine
nothingness: some end of all that is, some end of the universe, or some
boundary to existence. To my mind, such is incomprehensible. What
would lie beyond the wall of the universe? How could there even be
a boundary to it? Would there be space beyond the "wall?" And is not
even space itself something? Is it not at least a container for matter?
It seems to me if there is in truth a thing called infinity, and if this

is an infinite universe, it would follow that matter, space, and energy are all infinite—along with the elements that comprise matter or are themselves matter. It should follow then that all these elements are also infinite, no matter how rare or limited some of them might seem to be upon and within the microcosm we have named Earth. Gold is rare in some places, non-existent in some places, and abundant in other places. Why would not the same hold true for energy? Why should we be surprised to find that there is more energy near the sun than there is around the moon? Why should we be surprised that there might be greater energy around Sedona, Arizona, than there might be in say, Dumas, Texas, or that there is less energy in Ralls, Texas, than there is in Santa Fe, New Mexico?

The answer to such questions might lie within how we define or what we label as energy. If, when we speak of energy, we pertain to wind energy, then there may be more energy in Dumas and Ralls than in Sedona or Santa Fe. This might be counterbalanced in Sedona and Santa Fe by more intense solar radiation beaming down through less atmospheric pollution. Psychic energy or spiritual energy may be another item apart from what we consider to be physical energy, and like various other resources, it may be more concentrated in some areas than in others. I would presume there was more energy in the brain of Albert Einstein than in some other brains.

There are vast deposits of oil beneath the Permian Basin. There are none beneath the Llano Uplift—so far as is known. Just as there is oil in some places and not in other places, it could be that the Southwest has more magic and more psychic or spiritual energy than other areas. It may be that not everyone is able to tune the receiver to the proper frequencies; thus, they do not receive the energy or the products of the energy generated in some stations. Not everyone is able to locate where oil is; otherwise, there would be no dry holes drilled. The fact that both dry holes and productive ones are drilled can serve as an analogy to us about magic and spiritual energy. It can serve as an analogy to the literalness of psychic energy as well as the fabled imagining of such by some.

Just because someone cannot tune into the energy and forces of a Sedona vortex or tune into a spiritual presence in a certain place does not issue proof these things are not there. Think about this: there are some who feel absolutely no emotion when they hear *Rhapsody in Blue.* Others become spellbound. Some fall in love with those whom some others might find unattractive, or even repulsive. Similar considerations might apply to vortexes and to other places of psychic or spiritual energy. Do you believe in vortexes? Only you can know. Do I believe in vortexes? I have been in their epicenters. Do I believe in magical places? I have been surrounded by them. Do I believe in foreboding places? I have fled in fear from them.

II.
COMPELLING
EVIDENCE

THERE IS NO DOUBT in my mind there are places of energy, mystery, and power: places that draw both humans and animals to them—and perhaps spirits, too. There are places that compel people to visit and to even dwell permanently within their perimeters and boundaries. One can witness this, or much of this, around almost any playa, along almost any stream or river, or along various seashores or lakesides. There is not a great deal of mystery about this, and it is not so much a phenomenon as it is the simple reality that water is an absolute necessity for life as we know it. Water attracts life. Water sustains life.

Water is a catalyst for propagating life. It can be argued that water is the most important compound on the earth.

There are many terms for creative forces or for "The Creative Force." When what we term Nature, Existence, God, or The Great Spirit makes a presentation of water, and with that also makes a presentation of some prominent topographical feature, then there is likely to occur a place that we would consider one of great energy—or at least one of greater energy than some desiccated landscape we might label as mundane by comparison. Places of great energy can actually occur in the absence of water if there is some prominent geological feature present. One can witness this at Shiprock, New Mexico, where a prodigious volcanic neck protrudes some 1,800 feet above the surrounding desert floor of the Navajo Nation. This prominence is 8,085 feet above sea level, and it provides a magnificent contrast with the surrounding flat landscape. Such a presentation can also be seen at El Capitan, a marvelous limestone reef at the south end of the Guadalupe Mountains in West Texas. Such a presentation can be seen at Monument Valley, in the Navajo Nation where for eons the winds, blowing sands, and runoff waters have sculpted the earth's surface into wondrous red pinnacles and escarpments. All of these have become places of mystery and power and have beckoned to ancient people, some of whom left their rock carvings and paintings upon them. They beckon in this age to modern day tourists who have left their graffiti, beer cans, disposable diapers, gum wrappers and trash strewn about them. They beckon now to moviemakers who have endeared the golden west to millions who otherwise would not have even known about such beautiful sites. Fortunately, these places have also drawn many who love and take good care of all natural resources and natural treasures and who continue removing the litter left by thoughtless visitors.

If a prominent geological feature also has the presence of clear, cool water that is also potable water, then the place becomes even more enchanting, more charming, and we would label such a place as one that possesses great energy, or great power, or both. An example of such a place would be El Morro National Monument, also called Newspaper Rock or Inscription Rock. This site is in New Mexico and has been visited by humans for centuries. This is probably because of its large and deep *tinaja*. This pool has never been known to go dry. This *tinaja* is not a spring. It is a deep hole eroded by thousands of years of aqueous runoff from the surrounding area. It catches and stores much of this runoff and thus provides that precious substance necessary for life: clear, cool water.

Places of great energy and power are abundant throughout the Southwest. There are many in Arizona, where they seem to be distributed throughout the state. In the distant past, a huge meteor crashed into what is now called the Arizona Desert leaving a crater almost 600 feet deep and almost a mile in diameter. This ancient crater is some 50,000 years old and draws thousands to its view. It draws scientists, lay scientists, and the curious. It draws those who find it to be a place of energy and power, and it beckons to those who find it to be a place of intrigue.

Millions of years ago, rain was common on what is now this Arizona desert. Large trees grew. At some point in time the rains ceased, or rain became so infrequent that the climate changed and the forests died. The trees did not decompose or decay in a manner like much organic material does. These trees petrified. What actually happened was that the organic materials and hydrocarbons of the woods were replaced by substances such as jasper, quartz, calcites, or other minerals. They were replaced with such fidelity that even the cells of that ancient vegetation are identifiable. These rock tree carcasses now lie scattered upon the dry desert sands of Arizona. They attract thousands of tourists to a beautiful and curious "field of energy" now named the Petrified Forest.

The Grand Canyon, the forests of saguaro, and stands of organ cacti likewise draw both humans and other animals to them, even though with the cacti forests there is little, or no, obviously obtainable water. If the reader goes to Google on the Internet and types "Sites in Arizona," he will come upon a list of many places that might be considered places of energy. Many of these are compelling places, and some may be drawn to them without even realizing why they are.

The Superstition Mountains are another Arizona lure calling to the daring—and to those who like to defy the lore about them. There are legends of lost gold mines and treasures. There are legends stating that anyone who goes into those mountains will not return. Of course, people have gone into them and not returned, and people have gone into them and have returned. It is the mystery and the energy, along with the topographical beauty, that attracts people.

There are many more attractions in Arizona and in the Southwest than are listed here, and there are doubtless many not yet discovered, even by modern man with modern technological means. One of the most popular of well-known places in Arizona is Sedona. It is a magical place. It is a place of power. It is a place of energy and mystery. It is a place of great beauty—attracting photographers, painters, writers, and millions of visitors. There will be more about Sedona, its vortexes, and its special energy forces later.

III.
NEGATIVE
ENERGIES

IN DIAMETRIC OPPOSITION to the many wonderful and positive places of energy, there seem to be places that push people and animals away. These are places of bad energy, bad karma, and bad vibrations. We could refer to them as places of negative energy. I have felt them, experienced them, and witnessed my dog shying away from them. Sometimes I could not begin to tabulate the reasons for the foreboding feelings. For the past forty-five years, I have driven countless miles of highways and back roads. I would not undo or retract any of these odysseys, even if it were possible to do so. An overwhelming number of these places have been pleasantly meaningful, enchanting, awakening places, or places of spiritual experiences. Some, not many, but a slight few, have presented to me some feeling of dread, fear, or fright. Those have produced for me some foreboding feeling not grounded in reason, logic, or rational thought processes. I have considered that there may be some state of consciousness that psychologists might not have defined, such as a "mesoconsciousness." To my knowledge, there is no such word, but I have coined it because I have experienced something similar— something that seemed to be a state of mind between the subconscious and the conscious. In such states of mind, I have been in places that gave me the feeling that I just should not be there. I should leave— immediately!

At this point, I feel compelled to issue to the reader a disclaimer. I am not writing a scientific paper. I am sharing some things I have experienced, some things I have been told, and some of my thoughts and/or conjectures about places I have been. In no way am I attempting to mislead anyone, and I am not attempting to create some mysticism that might not exist. Let the reader read and make his own determinations.

During the past two decades, there have been various publications pertaining to mysteries and intrigue. These range from *Mutant Message Down Under,* to the *Celestine Prophecy,* and the *Da Vinci Code.* I promise you the writings in this book are light years apart from those just mentioned. There is no "mumbo–jumbo" herein. I have not been lost in the wilderness—unless it has been some spiritual wilderness. I have not been captured by aliens or aborigines, have not been on a space ship, have not seen little green men, and I do not use drugs. These writings are just reflections of things I have experienced and things I have considered about those experiences.

IV.

FORT McKAVETT

IN THE MIDDLE of the nineteenth century, the United States
government established a network of frontier forts across much of its
then unsettled territory. These were to protect pioneers engaged in the
westward movement, mainly from various peoples that these pioneers
had invaded. Many of these frontier outposts were abandoned soon
after they were established. Some are still abandoned, and there is little
or nothing left of some of these. A century and a half later, some have
been restored as historical sites. Some became townships and cities,
such as Fort Worth, Texas, Fort Stockton, Texas, and Fort Davis, Texas.
Some communities dropped the prefix as did Fort Mason, Texas, which

is now known simply as Mason. Others took on names that bore little or no resemblance to the former fort names, such as San Angelo (Fort Concho), Abilene (Fort Phantom Hill), or Fredericksburg (Fort Martin Scott). On and on the names go, close to fifty of them in Texas, and there are many more in other states.

One that intrigued me is Fort McKavett, situated beside the San Saba River in Menard County, Texas. It is in contrast to some because it has many stone structures yet standing. Early immigrants razed many other sites and used the stones for newer structures, as was done with Fort Mason where the heart of downtown is composed mostly of stones from the old fort.

Until the State of Texas decided to restore Fort McKavett in the late 1970s and early 1980s, it was an intriguing and haunting place. There was some activity within its boundaries, such as with the St. James Episcopal Church which was founded about 1874, some fifteen years after the fort was abandoned. In the 1890s, the Range Canning Company was established. It touted canned boiled mutton, but it was actually goat meat and not sheep meat. Then, much later on, there was a small café that sold beer and hamburgers. This was in one of the old stone fort structures. When the state began restoration, it evicted the proprietors, and they relocated to a small frame structure not too distant. I became friends with the operators and would often drive down from Odessa to visit with them and have a beer and a burger. They seemed like nice people: Ed McDaniels, his wife Arlene, and their young son, Patrick.

Theirs was somewhat of a hardship situation. Ed had lost both adrenal glands, could not do much work, and was denied social security benefits. Arlene was trying to earn a living for the family by operating the café, and Ed was doing what he could do, namely casting jewelry and unsuccessfully trying to generate sales for his products. Patrick had a heart condition diagnosed as a subaortic stenosis. They thought if they had more space to operate the café, things would improve. If they had additional sheltered quarters, they could have music events and thus sell more beer, confections, and burgers. They did not have the physical abilities to engage in construction work or the money to hire workers to do it. I told them I thought I could put together a barn raising. I did. I gathered some twenty helpers, among them Butch Hancock, Joe Ely, Jim Eppler, Spider Johnson, Wallace Bosse, Bill Murchison, Doug Lockard, Joe Brunelle, and several others whose names I am not presently recalling.

We built the structure in a day and a half, and the McDaniels then had a space for music and dining. About a month later, we had an event that featured Butch Hancock and Joe Ely. There was a really good crowd for such a happening staged in the middle of nowhere. All went well until Chic (a local Hispanic) and Ed McDaniels got into a brouhaha.

There was a very strong energy and a very bad energy at the edge of Fort McKavett, Texas, that night. The celebration of the new structure, the music, and the festivities all went down the drain. Chic had gone inside to purchase a six-pack of beer. Arlene had told him, "Now we don't want any trouble tonight Chic."

Chic replied, "Goddamn, Arlene, what kind of trouble?" Arlene's father, a former prizefighter, entered in. "You won't talk to my daughter like that!" and he spun Chic around and punched him out with a right hook. Chic hit the floor. When he recovered, Ed ordered him out of the store, waving a pistol and firing it while so doing. I remember hearing two shots. There may have been more. Chic ran to his pickup, followed closely by his Anglo girlfriend, who was running at his heels. Ed hollered, "Get out of here, you white trash!" The girl responded with, "You have a gun! We're gonna go get a gun too!" And away they drove.

And that broke up the party, so to speak. It broke up the music, the beer drinking, the hamburger eating, and everything else. I had taken a girl to the event that had never been around a gunfight, and she was terrified. I had not been around a gunfight either, and I was terrified. I did not want to witness one, either! Hastily, I summoned my friends to a very quick conference and told them I was heading over to the nearby ranch, where we had a bunkhouse awaiting us. They were quick to follow.

Because we were at the bunkhouse—several miles from the

scene of conflict (avoiding any possibility of the crossfire)—we had no way of knowing that the Menard County sheriff had taken Ed into custody. He took him to Menard, fined him, and perhaps incarcerated him for a few hours.

Back in the bunkhouse my group talked for a while, and then we all went to sleep. Sunday morning dawned, and Bill Murchison and I drove the five miles or so over to the Fort McKavett store. It was not yet 8:00 a.m. Beer cans, beer bottles, paper plates, napkins, pickles, buns and mustard, a few half-eaten wieners, plastic knives and forks, and a few other items littered the ground. We began picking them up and stuffing them in trash bags. It was a Sunday morning mess.

Arlene appeared. She was colder than hard frozen ice! She spoke, but barely. She was angry with us for not sticking around and helping with her husband's gunfight. This happened about 1978, and it is the last time I have seen any of the McDaniels. All the teamwork I put together, all of the construction, the music I arranged, the past visits made—any gratitude at all for these was completely overshadowed by her anger at our fleeing for our safety due to that impending gunfight.

Arlene was very attractive. She was also an angry and impetuous individual. She had a remarkably short fuse and a quasi-violent temper. A short time before this event, she had engaged in a conflict with the county commissioner, who resided in Menard, the county seat. Menard County had closed the public dump grounds at Fort McKavett. It was a big open pit and was quite ugly. It was a prime example of what can happen when a dump ground is not managed or regulated. Arlene protested the closing, asserting that she had no means of disposing of her garbage, and that it was the county's responsibility to provide her with a means of doing so. Motivated by her feelings of indignation, self-righteousness, and abuse, she went into Menard one night and dumped a load of trash upon the county commissioner's yard. She felt absolutely justified in doing this because he had not provided her with a means of disposal. This probably gave the sheriff a sizable bit of motivation for the hauling of Ed into court for firing the pistol over Chic's head. (This, and Ed's indiscretion when he fired shots above Chic's head with a crowd around, and at a place where alcohol was sold). The question of legality on Ed's part is a question subject to judicial debate.

Another one of the sad and negative things was that Doug Lockard bad-mouthed both Bill Murchison and me for leaving the scene. This added fuel to Arlene's displeasure and increased the enabling of her being a victim. (Of course, Doug did not stay for the gunfight either). He later told me that some day he would tell me why he "turned on us." To date he has not, and I have not given a fraction of a damn why since 1978. *Why* just did not matter.

It has been stated many times that no good deed goes unpunished. There is great truth to this. It is a paradox, and people attempt to mete the punishment in various ways. One way they do this is to shun someone or withhold communication. That is what happened with the McDaniels.

> Down the road of good intentions
> I have broke down a few times
> Done some things I hate to mention
> Trying to make the wrong seem right
>
> Before you try to help somebody
> Better know your reasons why
> Cause no good deed will go unpunished
> And those you help can make you cry*

* From "Down the Road of Good Intentions" Song lyrics by Gary Nicholson, Jay Boy Adams, & Bill Worrell. ©2010.

Most people in the McKavett area loved Arlene, thus Bill Murchison and I, once heroes of the community, were not thought of fondly after that unfortunate event.

There were other strange energies in Fort McKavett, too. During one of my previous visits, a Hispanic neighbor who lived next to the store came running and screaming about a snake in her stove and called upon me to assist her. I could not make a positive identification of the reptile because it was entwined in the burners, and I could see

neither its head nor its tail. It seemed to have markings similar to a copperhead. I did—very cautiously—remove it without harming it and found that it was a harmless bull snake. (Harmless to humans, that is, but not to rodents.)

I have a photograph of a young man named Midge Davis while he was in front of the store with a rattlesnake coiled upon his head. Midge died of a rattlesnake bite a couple of years later. He was playing with what is called a "high striker." It got him in the arm two times as he was attempting to remove it from a toolbox to show it off. "Let's get you to the doctor," said one of his friends.

"Let me have a beer first," he replied. After a few sips he said, "You boys better get me to the doctor. He got me worse than I thought. I'll be dead before you can make it, but try anyway." He was dead before they got him to the doctor.

One of the nearby residents had a reputation for picking fights. He (allegedly) would get his adversary on the ground and then gouge out his opponent's eyes with his thumbs.

Whatever became of Chic and his girlfriend is unknown to me. They simply drifted into some sea of obscurity.

I returned to the Fort McKavett Store twenty-seven years later with Wallace Bosse, who is now my neighbor on the Llano River and who was a major help with the 1978 construction event. We both agreed there is yet a strange and unsettling energy there. I have driven by a couple of times since without stopping. When I have done this, my thoughts have been that it is just one of those places I know I am not supposed to be. There is not a thing pulling me back to Fort McKavett, Texas. Well, I don't think there is. Wallace and I were talking about it and decided we might go back and drink a beer sometime.

MIDGE DAVIS WITH RATTLER.

THE STORE AT FORT MCKAVETT.

V.
SPIRITUAL
ENERGY

SOME PRAY. Some do not. Some do not even know what prayer is, it might seem. It might also seem that some think they know what prayer is when in reality—or unreality—they do not. Some consider prayer a waste of time. Some seem to have no connection with spirituality or claim not to have a connection with such. Some draw from prayer enormous amounts of energy. I am one of those. Others will issue testimony about all sorts of positive things that have resulted from prayers, including prosperity and abundance, guidance, direction, mind, reason, memory, peace, joy, love, and healing. They, along with me, will not be convinced that prayer is not a gatherer and a producer of energy, creativity, motivation, and even what some might label as magic.

I believe human behavior can present or create certain energies or certain moods about a place, be it a wilderness place or be it a place in some home or building, either within or outside a township or a city. This human behavior is sometimes benevolent, and it sometimes seems to be malevolent. Thus "good" and "bad" energies are created.

I have asked friends and acquaintances if they have had experiences with spiritual energies. As might be expected, some stated they have and some stated they have not. Some state they do not know if they have or have not. It seems obvious that pep rallies are staged to generate a type of spiritual or psychological energy—as are church revival meetings, monastic chants, occult ceremonies, organized marches for specific causes, yoga exercises, and various forms of meditations. I have no doubt about the existence of spiritual energy, be it good or be it bad.

VI.
ELECTRONIC
ENERGY

AMONG THE VERY INTERESTING ENERGIES and sources of power are those that people pipe into their homes. This is not in reference to natural gas or water or even electricity, although the latter is a conduit through which various other energies might flow—or at least it is the conduit through which some of the manufactured or electronically generated energies flow.

A major energy pipeline is that which is the keynote or theme in Ray Bradbury's novel, *Fahrenheit 451*. It is through this (not always but sometimes) monster that many families funnel into their homes, dens, and sanctuaries unbelievable horror, profanity, and almost indescribable vulgarity. Certainly, they sometimes pipe edifying and inspirational programs into their homes also, but my somewhat limited experiences with surfing through the channels lead me to believe the former outnumber the latter.

I have some of these electronic television devices, along with the little satellite dish that offers over 250 channel selections. I am not addicted to it, but rather, I use TV instead of the barbiturates that are advertised over it. I installed it so I could see my various friends in Nashville performing on what used to be TNN—back in the days before CBS bought it and clobbered it out of existence. After that, I discovered it has an amazing ability to put me to sleep.

The first time I selected HBO I was dumbfounded! In two minutes or so, I was bombarded by the MF word at least a dozen times by some stand up comedian. I then quickly switched channels to view some victim being ripped into pieces with a chain saw. Quickly, again I went to another channel to find the (then) governor of California blasting people into bleeding piles of flesh and blood with his Uzi.

I was so disturbed that I began surfing through my options. There was a self-appointed (and lying) preacher/evangelist telling me that God loves me and that He is going to send me to Hell to burn forever and forever and forever. Then he told me that sex is dirty, sinful, and evil, and that I should save it for someone I love. There was a commercial strongly hinting of adultery and infidelity with the admonition, "What happens in Vegas stays in Vegas." I mused that this may be true except for AIDS or other venereal diseases. Without a doubt, it is true for most of the monies laid upon the tables.

We pipe the energies of hate, rape, murder, robbery, assault, and profanity into our homes, and then we later wonder just what it is that is happening to kids these days. We pipe the words of congressmen, senators, past presidents, present presidents, their advisors, actors, celebrities, and assorted other personalities into our dens and our lairs, not knowing whether they are telling us the truth or not.

Recently I flipped through CNN, NBC, FOX, PT, and then back to CNN, NBC, FOX, PT, etc., until I became extremely distraught. All I saw was war, murders, suicide bombings, rapes, and larceny—or brown bears skinning and tearing live salmon into pieces and then eating them. I saw a brief section of "The Sopranos," where some man was beating up his grandmother and sacrificing her to the mob for money. It was horrible! I was distraught. I turned off the television set and thought I might read something soothing and reassuring. There is a Bible by my bedside. It is not that I believe everything that is written in the Bible, but I do find it a source of historical information. I also find in it some comforting words.

I let the Bible fall open where it chose to fall open, or where the force of gravity chose for it to open, and then began reading. It was the Book of Judges. I read for quite a while. I was a bit disturbed. I then allowed gravity to flip over to I Samuel 15 and Judges 19 and read some in those books. In these Biblical books people were killing their daughters, cutting their concubines into pieces, and scattering their body parts over Israel. They were chopping people "into pieces before the Lord in Gilgal." I closed the Bible and turned back to something not so violent on CNN. That put me to sleep.

VII.
A FRIEND
OF LONG AGO

THEY ARE AMAZING THINGS, those small remembrances, even if as things they are intangibles. But we remember with intangible things, like thoughts, those tangible things such as filling stations. "Filling Stations" is what we called them, "Service Stations" the metamorphosis, "Self Serve" the continuing evolution. Filling stations, as we knew them, are either gone, are memories, or are so rare that one can scarcely locate one.

The competition to sell gasoline was great four decades ago.

It is a bit strange that the demand for gasoline now is much greater, but the competition to sell it was greater way back when. Humble Oil, Sinclair, Gulf Oil, Texaco, and others advertised their fuels on radio and television. That was when gasoline was both cheap and abundant: before Hubert's Peak peaked, so to speak. Along with frequent spot ads, they also sponsored athletic events. Now, the competition to buy fuel seems greater than the competition to sell it. Gasoline was twenty-five cents a gallon back then. Add three or even four dollars to that now. Some complain at the price and then pay three times the amount for water.

There was interesting energy around filling stations in the 1950s. It was energy blended and mingled with sounds of sledgehammers hitting tire rims, pumps dinging with every gallon pumped, and the smells of gasoline, oil, and musky rubber. Busy energy it was, and it was usually energy of service and satisfaction.

In Colorado City, Texas, on the corner of Main Street and Locust Street, Bernie Grable sold gasoline for 25.9¢ a gallon at his Gulf Service Station. It was a *service* station. A typical total price tab for a fill up that registered on the pump might be something like $4.97. There were three wheels on those pumps, and they rolled in a manner similar to the pre-electronic slot machines. Each had digits from zero to nine. If a purchase exceeded $9.99, the wheels would roll to $0.00 and begin recounting. The highest number I saw on a gasoline pump until 1967 was seven dollars and some odd cents when Claude Patton filled his Pontiac sedan with ethyl gasoline at Muleshoe, Texas. Now days, when I fill my Expedition with fuel, the digital electronic device generally shows over fifty dollars, and I have seen it exceed one hundred dollars.

Along with the typically under-four-dollar purchase, Bernie Grable would "check under the hood." This meant checking the engine oil for both content and purity, checking the transmission fluid (if the car had automatic power transfer), checking the level of the battery water, and checking the radiator fluid. He would also check the fan belts for tension and wear and look for oil leaks, transmission leaks, radiator leaks, and water pump leaks. He would oil the things that in those days required such maintenance, such as the generator, the steering column, and the brake and clutch joints. Then he would clean the battery terminals and place a small drop of oil on both of them.

Bernie was not through at that point. He would check the air pressure in the four tires on the ground and also the pressure in the spare tire in the trunk. If a tire was badly worn or had some cut or defect, he would point it out and, of course, make an attempt to sell another one to the customer, reminding him of the hazards of driving on "bad rubber."

At that juncture he still was not finished. He had an old Maytag (or perhaps it was another brand) washing machine that had a hand-cranked wringer. The younger generation probably does not know what a wringer is. It is a "pre-dryer," so to speak: the predecessor of the "spin dry" cycle on a modern washing machine. Bernie kept the washer full of water with a chamois always soaking in it. He would run this very large, tanned piece of skin through the wringer and use it to wipe the bugs from the windshield and the dust from the other windows— both sides of them. Then he would wipe the rear view mirror clean as the proverbial whistle.

His routine was still not complete. With a small whiskbroom he would sweep the automobile floors. He did these tasks while the gasoline was pumping, and of course by the time he had performed all these labors, the pump had long ago shut off automatically. He would then milk the last possible drop of that abundant 25.9 ¢ per gallon gasoline into the car's tank, replace the gas cap, and give it a wipe with the chamois. A customer touching the gasoline nozzle was almost unheard of. In fact, Bernie took offense if someone did this.

After Bernie had performed these free services (that today we pay for—or cannot get), he would take money or a credit card at the driver's window. The customer usually sat through these procedures, and then Bernie would return to the window with change or credit card slips, complete the transaction with a smile, and ask the customer to "please come back."

Bernie proudly served our country during World War II. He also took pride in working and had little patience for indigence. He told me about a "deaf/mute" that came into his station. This was rather common in the 1950s. They were usually shabbily dressed, those "deaf/mutes," and they would, in complete silence, hand out a card that read, "I am a deaf/mute. I sell these cards for a living." Most often, someone would give them some coins, even in a depressed economy, and those beggars would then go on their way, attempting to sell more deaf/mute cards. Bernie had purchased a card from one of those people early one day. Then, toward closing time, a sharply dressed person came in and had Bernie fill the gasoline tank of a shiny new car. When payout time came, the man said, "I got a bunch of quarters for you, buddy!" Then he paid the tab with a handful of change. Bernie recognized that man, and afterwards when a supposed deaf/mute would come in, he would turn his back so his lips could not be read and shout, "You are the goofiest looking son of a bitch I have ever seen!" Then he would turn and face the person, smile, and simply shake his head, indicating "no."

There was only one thing Bernie liked better than selling gasoline and servicing vehicles. That was bass fishing. His latest catch was always—or almost always— swimming around in one of the two old-fashioned Coca Cola boxes he kept filled with water in the car wash room. He also had a passion for knives, and when he was not servicing customers' vehicles, he would hone them sharper than razors.

Old Bernie is probably up in Heaven right now, either bass fishing on some golden pond or servicing one of God's celestial chariots.

Every now and then as I pump my own gas—while the howling winds of winter chill my bones; as I scrape the crusty summer bugs from my hot windshield; as I trust to fortune that my tires have adequate pressurized air, and that the oil and everything else under the hood is o.k.—I think about Bernie Grable's Gulf Service Station. I think of the thousands of similar others that existed from Mexico to Canada and from California to New York. What a wonderful part of American life they were! I am bewildered that I just paid $3.85 per gallon for gasoline, view a $97.89 readout on the digital counter, then hang the nozzle in its cradle, replace my gas cap, climb back into my car, and marvel that there are not weeds growing in the dirt on my floorboard. My payment has already been recorded—with no hello, electronic thank you, or goodbye. Most often, I did not see anyone and did not speak with anyone. I mash a button, and glass cleaner is sprayed on the windshield as the wiper blades struggle to clear the dirty film from the glass and smear the guts of smashed bugs over the pane. Then they create a semblance of clear arcs in semi-vain attempts to remove the last of the remaining soaking insect carcasses from my vision.

As I drive back to the ranch, my reveries slowly change, and I think about my next painting, my next sculpture, or my next piece of music. Muse I do, and I think about my recent experiences while dealing with the energy of present-day corporate America. Today there is certainly some care-less energy in the service area of big business products. Ah! But there is some good energy, too.

Not long ago, I paid about $125 for an electronic ultra-sonic toothbrush. It ceased working after about three months. I sent it to the manufacturer and asked that it be repaired or replaced. I received a short and quite terse note stating that I must send a receipt. I did not have a clue where the receipt was. Thus I had no argument, and the company kept my toothbrush! Now that is some negative energy! Contrast it with that of Pure Digital Technologies, the makers of Flip video cameras.

I carried a Flip in a pouch on my belt. I was hiking a canyon—a tributary to the Rio Grande River—and it was strewn with large boulders. My walking staff broke, and I crashed on a rock. The camera cushioned the impact enough to prevent a broken hipbone, but the screen was smashed. I mailed it to Pure Digital, explaining that the damage was my fault, and I simply asked if it could be repaired. About two weeks later on a cold rainy evening, the UPS truck appeared at my studio. The package the driver left contained a new camera and a note telling me that the company wants every one of its customers to be completely satisfied, and that I did not have to provide it with a receipt, either. What great and good energy! I hope the sterling silver pendant sent to someone named Cisco at the Flip Support Team made its way there.

I purchased another electronic toothbrush about four months ago. It, too, quickly "bit the dust." I kept the receipt and wondered if I should even try. I did not. How this world could use some more energy like that of Bernie Grable's.

DOWNTOWN COLORADO CITY ON A QUIET
MORNING...MANY THINGS ARE GONE,
INCLUDING BERNIE'S GULF STATION. THE
BAKER HOTEL (LEFT) WAS A PRIME DINING,
SWIMMING, AND LODGING PLACE.

VIII.

A GHOSTLY ENERGY

DOES HUMAN BEHAVIOR affect the energies of and about a place? Some might argue that it does not. I am convinced it does. While thinking about this, and as I am applying those thoughts to various and certain places, I am remembering an incident relayed to me by a friend. He and some others were camping at a remote place in the Chihuahua Desert, not far from the Big Bend. Within the area there is an enormously high waterfall named Capote Falls. It is private property and almost impossible to access legally, or even physically, even if one has permission to do so. It has a surrounding landscape that is very dry. It is dry, parched, desiccated dessert. This beautiful waterfall is one of those ribbons of life: an unexpected oasis and a place that, without doubt, has drawn creatures and people to it for ages.

My friend found *atlatl* points (often mistakenly referred to as arrowheads), blades, and other ancient flint artifacts nearby. Then he and his friends discovered some equally ancient Indian graves, dug into them, and looted them of their artifact treasures. They bedded down at the falls that night beneath a clear starry sky. Within the *madrugada,* that time between midnight and dawn, there came the winds. They were unexpected winds, and they were also uncharacteristic winds, given the peaceful day it had been and the tranquil night that it was. Those were moaning, howling winds. They were chilling winds on a summer nocturne. They were winds that blew and scattered their belongings. They were winds that overturned their motorcycles. Those howling, chilling summer winds terrified their souls because they knew they had violated sacred grounds and had done things they should not have done. They had robbed the ancient graves of the dead. As suddenly as they came, the winds left. So did my friend and his companions. They re-interred the artifacts they had stolen, packed up, and made a hasty exit—with resolve never to return again. My friend told me it was a very ghostly energy.

RIGHT: CAPOTE FALLS.

IX.
THE MARFA
LIGHTS

NOT TOO FAR from the area of Capote Falls is the small town of
Marfa, Texas. Its most recent claim to fame is in the arts. The mystique
of this village has drawn writers, poets, painters, and sculptors into
the area. The visual arts have been especially affected. The Donald
Judd Museum was installed in a complex of abandoned United States
Army buildings. In this museum are the works of New York artist
Donald Judd. Judd constructed boxes of thick-walled aluminum and
Plexiglas. Until one visits this space, one would have little idea how

many variations could be created on the single theme of a rectangular, trapezoidal form. A person might be overwhelmed by the number of separate creations and the many simple variations Donald Judd made from the idea of a simple box.

Donald Judd certainly assisted in changing Marfa from a desiccated and dying small town to a very popular retreat. It is an artists' hangout now, but in the mid 1950s Marfa's fame was the movie, *Giant*. This film was based on Edna Ferber's novel by that name, and it starred some of the greatest Hollywood actors of the time, including Elizabeth Taylor, Rock Hudson, James Dean, Sal Mineo, and others. Part of the old movie set still stands—or is still crumbling—on the desert between Marfa and the almost extant town of Valentine.

For whatever reason, Marfa has become "the place to be," or rather, "the place to go to." If neither of those, then it is at least a place to go. Crumbling shanties bring premium prices. Deserted buildings have been remodeled and have become popular restaurants, galleries, and stores.

Marfa's single greatest notoriety may be what has been labeled "The Marfa Lights." These are a mystery that no one has yet solved, although myriad theories abound—from UFOs to espionage, to the United States military's secretiveness. If there is no espionage, military secretiveness, or little green men flying saucer-shaped crafts around, then no one knows (for certain) what the lights might be, why they are there, when they might appear, or virtually anything about them—except that they are mysterious. And if anyone really knows for certain what they are, that word has eluded the general public. Perhaps "knowing for certain" might be a state of mind that eludes the individual who, in reality, absolutely knows for certain: he just might not know for certain what he knows for certain. That is really not double talk. Just think about it.

People see the Marfa Lights at unexpected times. People go to Marfa to see them and do not see them. People sometimes go to see them and do see them. It is reported that these lights would appear in lines or rows in that vast desert surrounding the town. Sometimes they would move, other times they would be stationary. I once saw what appeared to be headlights traveling down the side of a nearby mountain. Viewing the sight the following morning, I discovered there was no road where I had seen headlights the previous night. A road at that site would have required an enormous feat of engineering and would have served little or no purpose.

A friend told me of seeing specks of light near Marfa one black night. They were far in the distance. He stopped to view them and almost instantly they moved towards him at an alarming speed—so fast that he hit the ground! There they were: large glowing lights right above his prostrated, fearful form. Then, suddenly as they had appeared, they vanished.

It is rumored that the U. S. Army Air Force closed its base near Marfa due to several nocturnal airplane crashes. It was reported that pilots would see airfield-landing lights where there was no airstrip, would attempt landings, and would then crash into the rough desert hills. I have not verified this, but it is—or was—local rumor and regional scuttlebutt.

There is some energy, some force that produces the Marfa Lights. There has to be— because light is energy. Like the Lubbock Lights, they remain a mystery, a mystery that seems to gather energy and beckon scientists, laity, and the curious. As one might imagine, business owners in Marfa are quite fond of the Marfa Lights.

Near Marfa and a bit to the south is the small West Texas town of Valentine. Its chief claim to fame is its name. Every year in early February, the postmaster is inundated with packaged mail—stamped and sent for the purpose of obtaining a Valentine postmark. It is then sent on its way to myriad places around the country with a February 14 Valentine postmark. This in itself is energy.

A nearby resident is an artist named Boyd Elder, who labels himself "Boyd de Valentino." Boyd rendered the wonderful covers for the Eagles' early albums—those fabulously painted steer skulls. His invented method of painting them is as interesting as are the visual products. Boyd is both a fascinating and a philosophical person.

Back in the 1970s, I was engaged in a conversation with him about existence, about God, about faith, and about various things related to metaphysical considerations. He told me about an experience he had one night when he was alone driving back to Valentine from El Paso some 250 miles to the west. As he often did, he began to contemplate his relationship to the spiritual realm and to God. In some feeling of desperation, he said to the Power above, "Just show me a sign. If you are really there, just show me a sign."

The words had scarcely left his tongue when he looked into the rear view mirror. The sky appeared as if it were on fire. He stopped the car, got out, and looked. He thought El Paso had been nuclear bombed. He stopped at the next pay telephone and made a call to see what might be going on. Nothing was happening back in El Paso. When he arrived at Valentine, no one knew anything about any kind of explosion, any lights, or any unusual happenings. He heard no reports on the radio of such, and the next day there was nothing relating to any unusual events in the newspaper.

Boyd told me, "I never asked that question again."

RIGHT: 2404 3RD PLACE. HOUSE
WHERE DADDY AND I SAW THE
LUBBOCK LIGHTS.

X.
THE LUBBOCK
LIGHTS

CHILDREN OF THE PRESENT times are so saturated with electronics they "have eyes to see and do not see. They have ears to hear and do not hear." They miss creating the memories those of my generation were able to store in the mind—rather than attempting to entrust such to a "smart phone." However, I might simply not understand the capabilities of a smart phone, and I can really have no idea about the memories someone might store due to using one. It does appear to me it is a drastically changed world from the one I knew when I was young. Maybe a phone might be able to store the smells of early morning spring flowers. It might be able to store the memories of catching the first fish, building a fort, or sailing through the air after jumping off a huge sand dune. I know it can photograph and video and thus store images, but some other person is required to operate it in order to capture many of these things. It is difficult to be fishing alone and take a video of the self catching the first fish or sailing through the air from a sand dune jump, and I am reasonably certain a smart phone cannot store olfactory sensations. I also suspect that one becomes so involved in operating the apparatus that the intensity of the various experiences is diminished. Then fifty years later, the smart phone into which these "memories" were entrusted will long be obsolete. A newer and smarter model with a different format will continuously surpass it, much as my old bag phone is dead and gone, much as my old Razor phone is dead and gone, much as my eight-track tape deck is dead and gone, and much as documents from my first Macintosh are not readable by my present one.

Other than real estate and the treasures of memory, there is little wealth nowadays that is not stored electronic data. Many people are so busy storing new electronic data they do not have time to review the data they have already stored. There is no time for them to listen to an old favorite stored on iTunes because, in the ever-abiding present, they are constantly downloading new things. It is koyannisqatsi. (Koyannisqatsi, sometimes spelled *koyannisquatsi,* is a Hopi word meaning "crazy life" or "life out of balance.")

Back in the days when my mind was a bit more *tabla rasa* than it is now, and when I was writing vivid memories onto its slate, there was much ado about the "Lubbock Lights." Mention of the phenomenon was common among much of the news media. The Lubbock Lights were a mystery then, and they are a mystery now. The mystery has yet to be scientifically explained.

On April 7, 1956, my parents came to Lubbock to pay me a visit. I was a 21-year-old hayseed kid from Colorado City, Texas, a small town some one hundred miles to the south. I was enrolled as a sociology major at Texas Technological College, now named Texas

Tech University. I was residing with three other boys in a small dump at 2404 3rd Place, a block east of the famous Hi Di Ho Drive-in. Late that evening, my dad and I were standing on the front porch engaged in conversation. For some reason we both looked up into the sky simultaneously. We both were momentarily dazed by what we saw. Above us a V-shaped formation of lights passed rapidly and soundlessly from the north to the south. We made our acknowledgements to each other about what we had witnessed. We discussed our intrigue, bewilderment, and wonder. We did not know what they were, only that they were strange lights in the nighttime Lubbock sky.

Twenty-one years later, my father died in Colorado City, Texas. One of my friends from Lubbock attended Daddy's memorial service. He had roomed with me in the same house on 3rd Place back in the 1950s. He was in the house when my parents were visiting and was inside when Daddy and I spotted the lights out on the front porch.

Daddy's death created a very sad time for me. That night we drove from C. City, as we called it, twenty-six miles south down to Silver, near Step Mountain, just to get away. I think we went in order for me to properly be with my sadness and to get away from other mourners. We may have gone because I remembered taking my dad to that place a decade or more before, and maybe, just maybe, I could rekindle that peaceful and joyful memory. It was a pitch-black night except for the wonderfully bright constellations and planets. Orion was overhead, and the Pleiades was gaining height. Bob and I talked for a long time as we were surrounded by the solitude and peaceful sounds of the desert.

"Something happened back in Lubbock I have never told you about," I said, and then I related to him the experience Daddy and I had that night on the front steps of our college abode those many years ago.

I said to him, "It was just as if you and I were to look up into the sky right now, like this…" and we both looked up. There they were again! A V-shaped formation of lights passed swiftly above us—strange, soundless lights traveling rapidly from the south to the north. We both saw them. It was April 7, 1977.

As I write this manuscript thirty-five years later, I am still in awe. What strange and eerie energy was that? Were those the famous Lubbock Lights Daddy and I saw in 1956? What was it Bob and I both saw 126 miles south of Lubbock in 1977? Did Daddy and I hallucinate simultaneously in Lubbock? Did Bob and I hallucinate simultaneously at Step Mountain? I do not think so. I do not think any of us hallucinated at either time, but I know I will never be able to fathom this mystery. I will never be able to explain it. I might not ever be able to convince any other person about what we saw. I can only write about it now, and interestingly enough, I am satisfied for those events and the Lubbock Lights to simply remain a mystery: an unknown energy and power.

XI.
FRATERNITIES

SOMEWHERE IN BETWEEN

In the sweet by and by
We will meet on that beautiful shore
In the sweet by and by
We will meet on that beautiful shore

We weren't grownups we weren't children
We were somewhere in between
Not too wise yet not too stupid
We were somewhere near sixteen

Old enough to be ready
Young enough to still get by
We did not have our set of wings
But we still tried and tried to fly

We thought the world had an end
Just past the edge of our hometown
God lived somewhere up in the sky
Sunday mornings He came down

Old enough to learn the things
Preachers don't want kids to know
Young enough to have pure dreams
And mostly do as we were told

We seemed to think we had nine lives
Were bullet proof would never ever die
Had no clue we lived on that edge
Some fell off old friends now long dead

Old enough to be ready
Young enough to question why
Guess that question remains unanswered
'Till the sweet by and by

We did not know life's fragileness
Wink an eye death brings a kiss
Now we try to teach our kids
Not to do the things we all did

We're old enough to be ready
Still young enough to feel alive
We finally got our set of wings
And here we are still trying to fly

That was life in our small town
Peyton place now all crumbled down

Looking back the truth is found
What goes around comes back around

In the sweet by and by
We will meet on that beautiful shore

This song tells a bit about how it was in Colorado City, Texas, when I was somewhere in between. I was in between being an adult and yet a child. In 1953 at age seventeen, I was graduated from Colorado High School. It was an interscholastic league class one-A institution of public learning in a town of about five thousand residents.

C. City, "The Mother City of West Texas," as the chamber of commerce called it, is in the heart of the Permian Basin. The economy was farming, ranching, and oil. Of course, there was oil. There is always oil, even where there is no oil. There were businesses to accommodate those engaged in these industries. There were the usual small-town establishments. There were three barbershops, several beauty shops, two variety stores, three grocery stores (plus a couple of small maverick ones), two operating movie houses (the Palace and the Ritz), one extant movie house (the Gem), three drive-in movie theatres, and three law firms (including my father's). There was KVMC, "The Voice of Mitchell County," 1320 on the AM radio dial. There were two Southern Baptist churches, one Methodist church, one Church of Christ, one Christian Church, one Assembly of God Church, one Seventh Day Adventist Church, One Presbyterian Church, one Episcopal Church—the oldest in the area—and one Roman Catholic Church. The latter was located in "the Sands," or what was referred to as "Mexican Town." Of course, this forced a certain type of integration in our fair town. That Catholic Church was *somewhat* integrated during Sunday Mass. I often wondered if the integration was physical, spiritual, or compulsory. The other churches were all-White congregations. Then there were the Black churches. Almost every denomination was represented in the Black part of town, and they were mostly located south of the T&P railroad tracks. There were, likewise, Hispanic denominational representations in the north part of town, the part located in "the Sands."

There was no such thing as an all-night convenience store. There was not an all-night truck stop. There was nothing open all-night except the Root Memorial Hospital, the police station, the Crawford Hotel, the Col-Tex Refinery, and the Kent Oil Station—a gasoline station at the east edge of town.

As is likely the case in every town, hamlet, and city anywhere, there were various elements of scandal and adultery, but we did not learn of these until after the passing of many years. They were shocking when they were revealed, and they were so intriguing that a few of us talk (and laugh) about them to this day.

There were about twenty-five filling stations, none of them being self-service. Two dollars worth of regular gasoline would just about "fill 'er up," and while the pump was running, the attendant would check the oil, check the tire pressures, wash the windshield, and sweep the floor of the vehicle. (As previously mentioned, Bernie Grable was not the only station attendant who did this, he was just the best and most thorough of those that did).

There were four restaurants that in those days we thought were quite snazzy. There were three drive-in restaurants. There was a primary school, an elementary school, a junior high school, and a high school. These were all White schools. There was a Black school that served grades one through twelve. It was a very nice facility and much more modern and up to date than the White school was. It was named after a very wealthy black man, "Eighty John Wallace." Eighty John is still legendary in Colorado City. There was a lake, and there was a Texas Electric power plant on the lake. The Col-Tex Refinery employed a large part of the population and also mercilessly polluted the Colorado River. There was a country club with a nine-hole golf course and a small lake. Although C. City was dry, the country club sold beer, whiskey and mixed drinks. It also had slot machines.

The statement that the town was dry is a fable, or at least partly fictitious. It was thirty-eight miles to Big Spring. That was the closest oasis. That is where the "non-drinking" church members obtained booze in a manner only they thought to be private. They stocked up on booze—usually in Big Spring, sometimes in San Angelo, and sometimes from the two local bootleggers. A large crosstie fence surrounded the bootlegger south of town, post-to-post, so no one could see what happened behind the timbers. The other was in the Sands and was operated by a Hispanic man who was kind enough to sell minors Lone Star Beer for two dollars a quart.

That was our town. That was the womb from which we were expelled through the birth canals of Highway 80 and Highway 101. Highway 80 became Interstate 20, and Highway 101 became Highway 208 beginning at San Angelo and ending at and connecting with Highway 84 at Snyder. These were the veins and capillaries that connected us to the rest of the world—to such faraway places as Abilene to the east, Midland and Odessa to the west, San Angelo to the south, and Snyder and Lubbock to the north. Past those places, the world dropped off.

There may have been a half dozen in my graduating class who had seen television. None of us had met the president, a movie star, or anyone really famous, but some of our classmates knew someone who knew someone who had met someone famous, thus giving us vicarious contact. All of us were green, but I was greener than most, and I was the youngest boy in my class. I was sixteen and seventeen when I was a senior, and I was competing with athletes who were two years older than I. But I was not too young or too green to be in love with Marquita Martin, the girl who made nightly pleas for me to never stop loving her—along with daily promises that she would love me forever.

Thanks to God and my parents, that was one of the shortest forevers in history. God's part in this was that He made Marquita one of the fickle kind. My parents' role in this was to ship me far beyond the place where our world ended, to a place 800 miles away, to Fort Collins, Colorado, where I was to study forestry at Colorado A & M College. Mother and Daddy knew the nature of the beast—or the bitch, so to speak—and their plan worked. Some 56 years later, I wrote a song about it. I wrote it in jest, of course.

THE LETTER

I opened up your letter one cold morning
I could not believe that it came from you
Like a slap in the face with no warning
Like a bolt of lightening from the blue

What happened to our vows of forever?
Your plea that I never stop loving you?
You walked out of my life and you were gone
And I could not believe that it was true

I guess love never really lasts forever
No matter how hard we may try
Like a flower it seems to bloom so sweetly
Then it folds, it withers, and it dies

I drove all night from Northern Colorado
Through half of Texas so I could talk to you
I drove 800 miles in disbelief
I knew what I read could not be true

I remember my knocking on your door
I remember your startled surprise
I remember how hard that door did slam
In my face like a ton of dynamite

Whatever happened to our vows of forever?
Your plea that I never stop loving you?
Back in those days I thought my life was over
But God always seems to take care of us fools

It seems like some old motion picture show
Ancient love, ancient memories, ancient vows
Now I thank God for the way that it all happened
And I thank God I'm not living those scenes now

I guess love never really lasts forever
No matter how hard we may try
Like a flower it seems to bloom so sweetly
Then it folds, it withers, and it dies

I did not want to go to college at all—for several reasons. One reason was that I was not a good student. This was likely because I had a severe hearing impairment, although I did not realize this at the time. I could not hear teachers' instructions or their explanations, but I simply thought I was not bright. Another reason was that I had a very good summer job at the Col-Tex Refinery, and I could have probably stayed on there full-time. The main reason was that all I wanted to do was marry Marquita and have never-ending sex. Such were small town ambitions for those like me. My parents had other ideas, and they won the battle.

After I received the "Dear John letter" from Marquita, I drove all night from Fort Collins, Colorado, to Colorado City, Texas, to affirm my denial of the truth. That was an 800-mile odyssey, just as the song states, and there were no interstate highways in those days. There were narrow winding roads that went through every hamlet and borough in Colorado, New Mexico, and Texas. There were a thousand traffic lights—each one red. Thus, fighting juvenile sleep and adolescent fatigue, I made it to Marquita's house. I knocked. She opened the door, gasped in disbelief and horror, and slammed it in my face. I have not seen her since. Somewhere she sleeps six feet below the surface of the earth, or so I have been told.

I was sort of a lost child at Colorado A & M. My advisor signed me up for twenty-one hours, on a quarter system at that. Like all men at Colorado A & M College, I was required to take ROTC. That was a miserable experience! What cruel and crusty energy that was! On bitter winter mornings I would leave my room before daylight to get to my first class. It would be dark when I returned to the house. I was lonely for Texas and for my Texas friends. I was cold, very cold. In those days of Vitalis and water, my hair would freeze into a solid mass while I was walking to class. My clothes were geared for Texas and not for northern Colorado, and hi-tech insulated gear was years and years in the future.

Cotton did not kill me, but it certainly chilled me to the marrow.

I made friends with my housemates and my roommate, and thus it came about that three of us—Jim Stroh, Gary Deter, and I—pledged Alpha Gamma Rho, a fraternity for Forestry majors only. Hazing was the word at AGR. Merciless hazing was really the word. The actives were macho sadists. They were despicable, in my opinion. They pounded the butt of Gary Deter even though he had boils over most of his body, including (I do not know for certain but I presumed) his rear end. At least he told me there were boils on his rear end. There were more actives than the one pledge that defended him—that was me— and even though I explained to the actives his condition, they continued to pound him. I stepped between them and simply stated something like this: "There are more of you than there are of me, and all of you are bigger than I am, but you're going to have to go through me before you hit him again." That was very careless energy, but I meant it, every word of it. They could have killed me, but they did not.

Part of my increasing delusions resulted from Gary's response. "Tex, you keep out of this. It's none of your business." They were playing what they called "ping pong" with Gary. He would bend over and get whacked by an active. He would then run over to another active, bend over, and get whacked again. They continued beating him, and I left the frat house and walked home in the cold, dark Fort Collins night.

My next delusion about Alpha Gamma Rho came when I learned that during a beer bust, the actives had moved around gravestones in a Fort Collins cemetery. After that, I took my pledge pin to the president of the fraternity, handed it to him, and said, "I quit! As far as I am concerned you all are nothing but a bunch of chicken shits, and I don't want anything to do with you!" That was the end of it with AGR and me.

The following year I enrolled at Texas Tech. What a relief it was to be a hundred miles from home rather than eight hundred, and to be at a much warmer latitude. Lubbock, Texas, was certainly no Garden of Eden, but it suited me much better than Fort Collins, Colorado, where I was one of only two Texans in the entire school. Physical education was a required subject for two years at Tech, so I took fencing for P. E. I had

a knack for it and was invited to try out for the varsity team. I made it
and was a varsity letterman for two years. I won a lot of medals in three
weapons. One day at practice the coach asked me if I had ever thought
of pledging a fraternity. I related some of my experiences. He assured
me that Phi Kappa Psi was not that way; his fraternity did not engage
in hazing and in such things as did Alpha Gamma Rho.

I gave it a try. I will give them credit for not moving gravestones
around—at least to my knowledge they did not. But the way they
treated pledges was worse, much worse. Pledges were required to obtain
ten signatures a week from actives. To obtain these signatures, pledges
had to perform tasks for the active members. Those tasks might include
cleaning an active's room, polishing his boots, or washing his car, even
when the weather had blown in a howling "blue norther." There were
pledge meetings, and there were meetings of pledges with actives.
There were scholastic requirements, and there were social requirements
including dating girls and attending dances and parties. In addition
to these things, there were "called meetings." These were meetings of
sudden and unexpected notice that were called by one or more of the
actives. And then, in addition to all this stuff, there was "Hell Week."
Hell week was a week of sleep deprivation and tormenting hazing.
Hell Week was the final torture before a pledge became what is termed
an active member of the fraternity—when he would then be able to
inflict the same misery on new pledges. Hell Week was at the end of a
semester and during final exams. It took a lot of time and energy to be
a pledge. It took a lot more time and energy than I was willing to give. I
did not understand just what it was that the poor suckers who endured
all of the insane manipulations of the actives thought they needed to
prove. I knew for certain I had nothing to prove, either to the other
pledges, to the actives, or to myself. I did not make it to Hell Week. I
attended one called meeting and then turned in my pledge pin.

That infamous and notorious called meeting was set in a
classroom of the administration building. We were given an empty flour
sack and then ordered to rake all the chalk from the blackboard trays
in every classroom in the administration building. We were to rake the
chalk into the sack and then meet in the parking lot. There we were
blindfolded and placed into the trunks of the actives' cars. During the

dark drive to wherever, the drivers performed doughnut turns, u-turns, and various stops and starts in attempts to confuse us and perhaps to nauseate us. After a while, we were "untrunked" in some remote pasture. Then, out came the case of Garret's Snuff, the jug of mineral oil, and the Dixie Cups.

The actives dumped a can of snuff in a Dixie Cup—one can of snuff and one cup for each pledge. They filled the cups with mineral oil, stirred the contents, and ordered us to drink. If we developed emesis, we were to regurgitate into the cup and drink the vomit. We were ordered to run in figure eights until we were winded. From there it was back into the car trunks.

Can you believe that? Can you believe that those stupid pledges drank that stuff? Well, nearly every one of them did. Every pledge drank the mineral oil and snuff except for me! I told the actives I would not drink it. They told me I would. I told them I would not. They told me I would. I told them they far outnumbered me, but even so, there were not enough of them to make me drink it. I did not, and they did not make me. I had trouble believing the others did what they did. I was informed that some of the pledges had to wear sanitary napkins the following day because they had the scours so bad.

We were dumped out on Highway 84 West near Shallowater, Texas, where we were marched onto the railroad tracks. We were instructed to mark every cross tie with chalk and to number every tenth one—all the way back into Lubbock. Then the actives opened more beers and drove away.

We were some fifteen miles from Lubbock. It was winter. There was a howling, bone chilling, freezing blue norther blowing, and the temperature was in the twenties. We were already numb from the previous initiations and the rides in car trunks, and there we were—a flock of brainless, miserable, freezing sheep—marking and numbering railroad cross ties. On that cold winter night, I walked away from the gang of sheep over to Highway 84 East. A few pledges followed me, and we hitched rides back into town.

We had been told if we missed a class the following morning

we were out of the fraternity. I did not miss the one class I had the following morning, but the teacher did. It was my physical education class. It was fencing. The teacher was the fencing coach who had persuaded me to pledge that sadistic group called Phi Kappa Psi. He did not show up for class! But he was not kicked out of the fraternity. After all, rank has its privileges.

One week later we were again ordered to convene for another called meeting. Our instructions were to wear old clothes we did not mind ruining and to meet at the administration building parking lot. I was absolutely fed up to my gills with nonsense and cruelty. We could have been engaging in something constructive, something of community or collegiate service. I did not go to that called meeting, but I heard reports from some who did.

They were again placed in the actives' car trunks. They were driven south some forty miles past Post, Texas. There, in the dark and desolate canyons of the Caprock Country, they were divested of money, wallets, watches, and any lighters or matches. They were separated and stripped. Their clothes were dunked into a barrel of livestock molasses. Wet, soggy, and sticky, they were tossed upon the ground. Each was on his own to get those wet and soggy clothes back on and to find his way to whatever road or highway and to make his lonely, cold, molasses-soaked journey back to Lubbock.

It was still winter, and it was still cold. Some of the boys had bleeding cuts and sores by the time they got back home, which was well after dawn for some of the less enterprising ones. While all this was transpiring, I was sleeping comfortably in my warm cozy room at 2219 13th Street.

Those that endured the torment are eternally bonded as brothers of sorts—or so they claim. I became bonded with a different ilk, one that neither inflicted such torture nor acquiesced to it. It was to the sardonically smiling, arrogant bastard president of Phi Kappa Psi that I returned my pledge pin a few days later. The fencing coach was a reasonable person, and he did not condemn me for my actions. For two years I was a varsity letterman in foil, saber, and epee, and then I quit the fencing team. That is another story.

JIM RABBY'S PALETTE.

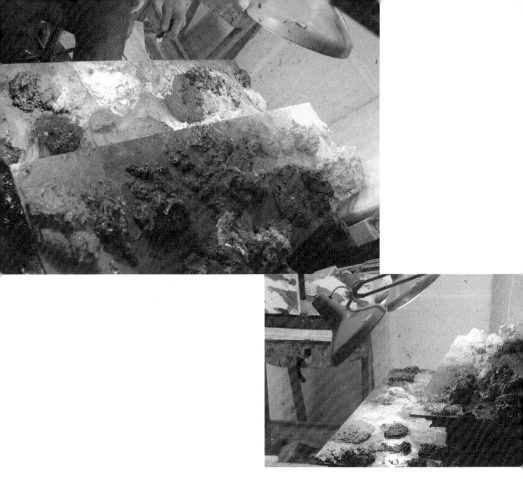

XII.
ENERGY OF
AN ARTIST

PRACTICALLY EVERYONE speaks about energy these days. It is
a topic on the news. It is a subject printed in the papers. It is an item
discussed in the congressional halls and the White House. The fear of
losing availability of fossil energy, or depleting the reserves of fossil
energy, has spawned conflicts and wars. But there is much more to
energy than oil, gas, coal, solar collection, and wind generators. People
feel energy when they visit my studio. I feel various energies from
various visitors. Usually it is a good energy. Sometimes the energy is

a strange energy. Sometimes the energy is not so good. I feel various kinds of energy when I visit the studios of other artists. Sometimes it is exhilarating. Sometimes it is calming. Sometimes I want to leave. I feel energies in my own studio. It is pleasing and usually satisfying energy I experience there, and I often marvel that things created in this space find their ways into collections across the continent and even around the world. I am humbled and in awe that this happens. As it may be with any artist, it is somewhat as if a source of energy travels from the studio to some distant place: the work not being simply some static piece of art, but rather an item of energy itself—energy that is in flux of some sort.

A few times, I was in the studio of a very well known and recognized Santa Fe artist. I was surprised each time I was there because he was painting in front of a television set. I was aghast! He was painting in front of a television set, dividing his time between his palette and canvas and the screen of the TV! The speakers were so loud I could not carry on a decent conversation with him, and I could not concentrate on anything other than wanting to get out of that place! Each time I went into his studio, I got out as fast as I could (and I only entered it due to a business relationship). I was amazed that he could create what seemed to be such spiritual work while he watched programs of violence and distressing newscasts.

This was Frank Howell's studio. It was a leased space in a strip mall. It was Frank who gave me my really big break in Santa Fe. I was with the C.G. Rein Galleries in Santa Fe, Houston, Scottsdale, Denver, and Minneapolis. Rein did quite well for me, but his policies of harsh and rigid control did not work well for a creative and industrious artist, or especially for one with a lot of ambition. That is the reason Frank left him and established his own operation. That is why Frank knew I would be constantly squelched with Rein—and with Frank I could blossom. That case was proven, and I am grateful to both Clayton Rein and Frank Howell for the opportunities they presented to me.

Frank's studio was not necessarily bad energy, but it was certainly not appropriate energy for me. It must have worked for him because he was quite successful and very well known. To me, daytime television is depressing. For me it would be a thief of time and energy. I often use TV at night rather than a barbiturate. That is about the extent of it for me. I sometimes use it to maintain a perspective about how wonderful my life is here at New Art compared to how it is in too much of the world!

On the subject of studios and studio energy, one of the most energy-potent studios I have yet visited is that of Santa Fe artist Jim Rabby. His palette of oil paints is so spread out and so large that it resembles a salad bar more than a painter's palette. There are mounds and mounds of paints spread upon a large table. Some of these globs are as large as melons. There are also rolls and rolls of fine Belgium linen canvas and stacks and stacks of stretcher bars and framing stock. There are racks and racks and racks of canvases in various stages of completion, each with a tag stating what has been done to the piece and what remains to be done. These occupy several rooms in a large two-story structure.

It takes about a year for Rabby to complete a painting. This is due to the wonderful and luscious thickness of his oil paint applications. Impasto does not even begin to describe his technique. He is an amazing person, too. He had polio when he was age nine months. He has had three full hip replacements. Sometimes he uses crutches, yet he stretches all of his own canvases and builds all of his own frames. He constructs many of the crates for shipping also. As I write this, I speculate that there are far more than 1,000 Rabby paintings in various stages of progress, each with that sticky tag stating what has been done and what remains to be done.

Rabby goes to bed before sundown and arises hours before dawn to begin his day's activities. He is usually up and working by 2:00 a.m. I once told him, "Rabby, the problem with you is that you just have no work ethic!" Every time I leave his studio, I leave filled with energy and with the desire to create. I think almost anyone would be pleased to experience the energy of his surroundings and to soak in the energy from a Jim Rabby painting. It is such beautiful and inspiring energy from beautiful and inspiring paintings. That is more like what the world should be viewing and talking about rather than so many negative things.

XIII.
ENERGY FROM
GOOD ADVICE

THERE IS ENERGY SURROUNDING ADVICE, always, both good advice and poor advice. I have had a good share of both, as have many people. Some of the bad advice concerned real estate. Some of the good advice concerned real estate. Some of the advice, both good and bad, concerned asking various girls out on dates. The most outstanding two pieces of advice that I recall came from Bob Beasley and from W.D. Noel. Bob was the district sales manager for the Lubbock office of New York Life Insurance Company. W.D. (Bill) Noel was the founder and

CEO of El Paso Products located in Odessa, Texas.

After selling insurance for the Equitable Life Assurance Society of the United States—for six miserable months—I told them to go to the hot place below and affiliated with New York Life. So much better, it was. I stayed with them for some three plus years then resigned and devoted my life to studying art, creating art, and earning a teacher's certification in art education at the secondary level. This was in Lubbock, at Texas Tech University. The way this came about was that one day Bob Beasley asked me why I did not quit the insurance business, go back to school, earn a degree in art, and be an artist (i.e. quit the insurance business and do something I really wanted to do). I told him there was nothing more that I would like to do, but I countered with, "Do you know how long that would take? That would take me another three years. Do you know how old I will be then?"

"How old?" he asked me.

"I would be thirty-three years old by the time I finished that!"

"Oh! I hadn't thought about that. There was a long, silent pause, then he asked, "If you do not go back and earn a degree in art, how old will you be in three years?"

So, you know what I did. Three years later, I was teaching art at Odessa College. Some few years later, after I had earned certification and a masters of fine arts degree, I was at a party hosted by some very wealthy and influential Odessa citizens. I affectionately refer to them as my "Little Old Ladies." They were the wives of lawyers, doctors, and oil company moguls. That occasion enabled me to ask W.D. Noel a question that had been haunting me for many years. Here is how that conversation went:

"Mr. Noel, I have such great respect for you. You started with little or nothing, and you built an empire. You are so very successful. I have contemplated and contemplated about the ingredients of success. I have thought that hard work is one of these. I have thought, surely, intelligence is another of these. But something is missing. (I knew I was at least reasonably intelligent, and I knew as far as work was involved, there were few who could out-work me.) I know there is something else involved, and I just cannot figure out what it is."

He responded somewhat as follows. "You are correct. Intelligence is absolutely a necessary item, and so is hard work. But there is another ingredient. That is risk. It is a reasonable, cautious, carefully calculated and non-capricious risk."

The conversation with Bob Beasley was in the late 1960s. The conversation with Bill Noel was sometime in the latter 1970s, and I spent another ten years or so trying to figure out what my risk was—my "carefully calculated and non-capricious risk." Then, suddenly one day, it was staring me in the face. I took the risk. I am here to testify that if one adds another ingredient to the mix, that being integrity, things are much more peaceful than I imagine them to be with some who do not exercise integrity. I can testify there is great energy and even power surrounding that "reasonable, cautious, non-capricious, and carefully calculated" risk. From my perspective, limited or not so limited, I think that just because one is cautious, non-capricious, and carefully calculating does not insure success, because there are so many "wild cards" in this world. One thing seems obvious: if the risk is not taken, then although one might "get by," he or she will likely not soar. Sometimes taking the risk works, and sometimes it may not work. In my case, it did.

XIV.
GIVING AND RECEIVING

"REMEMBERING THE WORDS the Lord Jesus himself said: 'It is more blessed to give than to receive.'" This quote is from the New Testament. It is found in Acts 20:35 and was likely written by the Apostle Paul. But you will not find those words "the Lord Jesus himself said" in any red-letter edition of the New Testament. Words printed in red are supposedly the words of Jesus. Paul probably just wanted to convince people they should give money to further the cause. Even back in those days, there was a great emphasis in religious circles about money. I think giving is an act of kindness, but we need to be so careful about what we give to others. Our good intentions can sometimes be offensive, and when they are, it does not generate good energy. I remember a girl telling me she was going to give me a great big kiss because I had done something to help her. I fled in terror! It was not quite as bad as Freud's account of the Devil's flight from the woman exposing herself, but I definitely did not want a kiss from that girl!

Sometimes I have guests. Sometimes they just suddenly appear, dropping by with no notice whatsoever. After a few minutes some visitor might say something like, "I've got the flu so bad I can hardly see straight," or, "I've had the worst cold for a week now," and of course it is then given to me!

I wonder how many times I have given someone something with which he or she had no reasonable way of dealing. I suspect I have done this many times. My heart was pure and my intentions were honorable—at least I thought so—but the gift was a burden. I wonder how many times?

I have a great deal of trouble or difficulty in disposing of things gifted to me, and I have a lot of them. I have stacks of wicker baskets, and I have never liked wicker. I have various items of clothing I have not worn one time. I have ceramic vases, books about how to become a perfect person, books on how to deal with every negative thing imaginable, books on how to grow a garden in a corner of your living room that will sustain 100 people, books on the real meaning of the Bible, books on our poor pathetic dying planet. I have plastic flowers, ceramic boots, paintings, sculptures, and even items of food that have been gifted to me. Such food gifts might include semi-raw, smoked pork ribs marinated in goat blood; sushi and smoked squid, smoked calf testicles stuffed with jalapeños, and items canned in Asia. All of such things people have brought to me as gifts, and the givers meant well.

Sometimes I just load these things up in plastic bags. I drop them off for the homeless wanderers to discover and perhaps to feast upon. I usually include a few bottles of beer or a bottle of wine and some chips in case whoever discovers the cache is not fond of sushi, jalapeño stuffed testicles, or smoked pork ribs marinated in goat blood.

Not too long ago I had a visitor, a dear friend. She brought another person with her. This person later sent me an item in appreciation of the New Art experience. It is one of the most grotesque things I have ever visualized, and it possesses the most unpleasant tactile experience imaginable. It is crudely fashioned and has pockets where pebbles that were inserted into it have fallen away, leaving ridges so abrasive and sharp they will easily cut through and tear the skin of human hands. I wonder, was this some kind of joke? Was it some kind of slap in the face? Was it an act of sincerity? And most of all, I wonder what I am to do with the object. I was on the verge of tossing it when I learned that the person who gifted it was to soon pay me another visit. I set it in a prominent place. She was delighted to see it.

I also wonder about the guilt! My guilt. I even wonder about the guilt of my writing these things. Guilt is a non-productive energy, so I am simply going to forgive myself for even mentioning this and go on to something else. I hope that you do the same with your guilt.

These days, I usually refrain from giving someone something unless I am asked to do so. Even then, I sometimes beg off.

XV.

A SANTA FE
AMBIENCE

THERE ONCE WAS A STORE on Canyon Road in Santa Fe, New Mexico, "The Land of Enchantment." It was like a candy store for artists. It was enchanting, mesmerizing, and full of creative energy. It served artists in Santa Fe and across America. It was such a delightful treat passing through its doors, even when I was caught up on art supplies. I would go there just to be there. I loved it!

The store was named Artisan, and it was founded by Bill Banta and Jack Young. Both Bill and Jack were Houston businessmen, and

Jack was also a painter. Both of them fell in love with Santa Fe and the energetic magic of the village, so they moved there, leased a building, and founded this fabulous art store. That was back in 1975.

Artists from everywhere were drawn to 558 Canyon Road. It drew both the professional artists and the amateur artists. It even lured the noted and reclusive Georgia O'Keeffe through its doors. I loved viewing the never-cashed check made out and signed by this famous woman. It was framed and hung on the wall behind the checkout counter. It was written on May 1, 1978 for $4.93. This was for a tube of Monestial Blue oil paint.

Georgia would come into the store early—around 8:30 a.m.— even though the business did not open until 9:00 a.m. Bill and Jack would indulge her and her eccentric ways and open the door for her. They said she often brought back or returned what seemed like more than she purchased. This is such an interesting revelation of a very small part of O'Keeffe—a woman who was, and still is, probably the most famous of all American women painters. Her estate was surely affluent enough that she need not return small change items. But her eccentric ways are what made her the Georgia O'Keeffe that only a part of the world knows! Or, they are a part of the eccentricities that made her what she was.

Artisan on Canyon Road was a fairyland for the artist. There were uncountable numbers of every kind of brush imaginable, and at almost every price imaginable, too. There were brushes priced under $1.00. There were brushes priced for over $1,000. There were jars and bottles and tubes of oils, watercolors, and acrylics, and these by the thousands. There were stacks of pastels, and there were grounds and pigments and pens and pencils and papers and tablets. There were sketch boards, sculpting tools, matte boards, books, canvases, and anything else an artist might need or desire.

Bill Banta died in 1994, and Jack Young died in 2003, leaving the store to Ron Whitmore. That Artisan store on Canyon Road was a place of tremendous energy, and it was positive energy. It closed on September 30, 2005, after more than thirty years of service. Ron and Karen Whitmore, the owners of the business, along with their

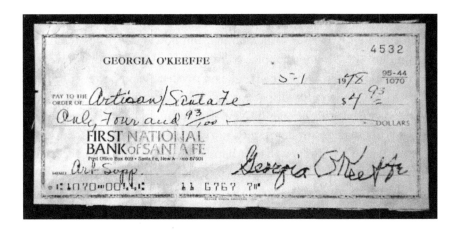

UNCASHED GEORGIA O'KEEFE CHECK.

employees are as sad as the rest of us about this. They just could not keep pace with the demands of the new heirs and owners of the building that housed that business, and those people would not sell the property. They raised the rent to astronomical figures, wanting as much rent or lease money just for the adjacent parking lot as Ron had been paying for the entire building. Ah, but greed creates its own energy too, and for a year or more, the premises sat vacant without producing anything for the owners except upkeep and taxes due.

Upon the closing of this art store, Ron gave scores of thousands of dollars of inventory to schools in New Mexico that are in quasi-poverty. He gave supplies to schools in Mississippi that were devastated by Hurricane Katrina. He gave me boxes of art supplies to take back to schools in Texas. That was the last time I passed through the doors of Artisan on Canyon Road. The place that was formerly such a place of energy was now scarcely recognizable. Gone were the tables and shelves and benches that held the magic and the treasures. Gone were the books and magazines and publications of art. Gone were the charming sales attendants. Gone was everything, except for scraps of paper, splinters of wood, and various other items strewn about. Things once prized were but litter now, litter that was scattered about the floors. It was like a looted tomb that was void of the delights and fineries it once contained.

Artisan is not gone; that particular space is now gone. Ron and Karen still own Artisan in Albuquerque, and now on Cerrillos Road in Santa Fe. These wonderful places will grow and grow in their own energies, and they will eventually take on mysteries and powers of their own. The old Canyon Road space at 558 became a gallery and for a while took on a different energy. New people entered its doors, never knowing the magic, power, mystery, intrigue, fascination, and energy once contained within its walls. Perhaps a few visitors had the necessary receivers to tune in to the spirits and the ghosts now mourning—ghosts and spirits that will surely always visit or haunt that space. There was a sign in the window that read "For Rent." Then someone rented it. Before long, there was another sign in the window that read, "For Rent." Someone will again rent the building and establish another gallery within the space. In all likelihood, there will someday again be a sign in the window that reads, "For Rent."

I have not been inside the remodeled premises since that day I picked up the supplies to give to schools in Texas. I will return some day, and I will scarcely see the paintings hanging on the wall. I know I will reminisce and dwell in a sort of past tense. I will be tuned in, tuned in to the spirits of Bill Banta, Jack Young, Georgia O'Keeffe, Tommy Maccione, and the scores of legendary personalities that painted their way to prominence in Santa Fe.

XVI.
EL SANTUARIO
DE CHIMAYO

NEW MEXICO IS THE LAND OF ENCHANTMENT. It has been
for eons. That is why Native Americans settled there. Enchantment
and adventure lured the Conquistadores to the New World—to what
is now Florida in search of the Fountain of Youth, and on westward to
search for riches and the Seven Cities of Gold. They came to engage in
searches for these things, to establish territory for the king of Spain, and
to make religious conversions for the Church. They were in the service
of God, the king (or queen) of Spain, and the self. They regarded that

EL SANTUARIO DE CHIMAYO.

to serve one was to serve each, so serving the self was to also serve God and the crown and a most noble thing to do.

There are vast amounts of lore and history in New Mexico. The feelings of enchantment, mystery, and energy, along with the places of power, give reason as to why so many people visit this majestic country. The novel *Ben Hur* was written in Santa Fe or partly written there. The state's first Governor, Lew Wallace, penned portions of it on the north side of the plaza. Santa Fe continues to be a hangout for actors, poets, writers, painters, sculptors, filmmakers, philosophers, and what might be labeled just ordinary people—some two million of them—visiting this village each year.

There is a place of incredible energy and power a few miles north of Santa Fe. It is near that part of New Mexico where Robert Redford filmed *Milagro Beanfield War,* the movie based on a novel by John Nichols that surely must be the *Fiddler on the Roof* of the Southwest. Nearby is the village of Chimayo. There are at least two meanings the name of this village has. One is of Tewa Indian origin and means "Hill of the East." The other meaning is "Best Obsidian." These days Chimayo is mostly famous for its weavings, its restaurant, the famous Casa Escondida B&B, and for its notable and historic adobe church. The church is *El Santuario de Chimayo.* Every year around the time of Easter, pilgrims journey to this holy and sacred edifice. They come from near and far, even from hundreds of miles away. Many possessing strong faith have limped long weary miles to get to this sanctuary. Those seeking to be healed often do not come to this place riding in vehicles or upon horses; rather, they come on foot—walking and sometimes crawling. They come on crutches, and they come in wheelchairs. They come alone, and some come with friends, relatives, and families. They come to *El Santuario de Chimayo* to pray, to light candles, and to be healed.

Some who hear about "miracle healing" are skeptics. Others believe the stories of healing, having themselves experienced it. There are mounds of testimonies from those who have been healed in this church. If you travel to The East Hill or to Best Obsidian and visit this place, you will find, in a room adjacent to the sanctuary, piles and stacks of crutches, canes, wheelchairs, and braces left by those who visited this special place of spiritual energy. They traveled there using those items—those crutches and canes and wheelchairs—and left without them.

There are some souls who know doubt and fear can maim. There are some who know that Belief and Faith can heal. Candles burn in the church, candles lit by believers. I have lit candles in this church. I will light candles in *El Santuario de Chimayo* again.

XVII.
THE GALLINAS RIVER

IN 1969, or about that time, I was taking a watercolor course at Texas Tech under Dr. Clarence Kincaid. It was a summer class meeting daily for six weeks in Taos, New Mexico. I had a job and was working in Lubbock at the time, so I could not live away from that job. I made negotiations to take the course under an "arranged" situation. I would drive from Lubbock to Taos every few days, meet with the class, and have a critique. On one of these sojourns, I took my friend Glenn Bradley with me. After my doings in Taos were done, Glenn and I went camping on the Gallinas River at a place northwest of Las Vegas, New Mexico. It was a rather tranquil and peaceful experience as I recall, and at that time I had absolutely no forewarning of experiences along that stream that would happen in the future. Two of the most haunted, haunting, and eerie of things I have experienced both happened at the same place on the Gallinas River in northern New Mexico. Both occurred less than a quarter of a mile from that peaceful place where Glenn Bradley and I camped.

Even though they may hold great fascination and intrigue, some areas of this state are to me quite foreboding. These feelings have come about while actually being in these places and not from any preconceived notions about them. Some of these areas are *Penitente* strongholds, and I think that is what holds their foreboding energy for me. The Penitentes are remnants of cults that originated in the days when the territory that is now New Mexico was first being occupied and settled by Spanish priests and by the Spanish Conquistadores. They brought with them what they thought, what they stated, and what was reputed to be Christianity. Remember, their mission was to serve God, the king, and themselves, and most often they made no distinction regarding which was the most important among these. Serving the Self was to serve God. Serving God served the Self. Serving the King served both of these—and serving both God and Self served the King. There was no way to lose in that convenient arrangement, and it was a most clever invention when blame needed to be cast.

The so-called Native Americans' descendants, the blend of Spanish and American Indian, have been labeled *Mestizos*. They took the teachings of the padres so literally and so passionately that they developed occult ceremonies reenacting the crucifixion of Jesus. They reenacted the crucifixion literally, except they usually halted the rituals short of breaking the leg bones, piercing the side, and short of allowing the candidate to expire on the cross. There was and is no greater honor among the Penitentes than that of being selected to represent the Christos and His crucifixion. The Penitente ritual includes the candidate being flogged while carrying a cross through the legendary twelve stations, as did Jesus, and then to be nailed (or at least strapped) upon that cross, as had been done to Jesus, and then for it to be staked up upon a hill, just as had been done with the Messiah.

Although this practice has been frowned upon by laity and clergy, and although the government has outlawed the practice, it remains a secret ritual in some areas. Those who engage in these occult, ritualistic ceremonies do not want outsiders observing them. One who makes attempts to do this might not return to anywhere. He might simply "vanish," or so the lore goes.

I once befriended a man who was caretaker of the church at Las Trampas, a village on the High Road from Santa Fe to Taos. He confidentially took me into a vestibule that was splattered with Penitente blood. There was dried blood on the floor, the walls, and the ceiling. There was age-old blood, along with relatively new blood. Blood had been splattered in this room through the decades: the result of floggings and flagellations given to candidates to enable them to suffer the same pain, agony, and misery that had been suffered by Jesus Christ. Lee Roy, the caretaker, told me some of the floggings were self-administered flagellations. Some people seem to love suffering, both for themselves and for others.

This practice prevails to this day in isolated locations and is still prevalent in some areas of Mora County, New Mexico. There is a Penitente group or cult up the Gallinas River, which is a beautiful, clear cold water stream. It is in this area, just a few miles above Las Vegas, New Mexico, where two families from Odessa, Texas, the Burgers and the Fursts, purchased a cabin. It was one of those rare buys, the buy of a century so to speak, and one that was made initially with a promissory note on a brown paper bag— along with a few old sweaty and odiferous twenty dollar bills that Gillette Burger kept stashed in his shoe, just in case of emergencies. The emergency occurred, and Burger made the deal.

Burger, a veterinarian, and Furst, a pediatrician, were both in my pottery class when I was teaching at Odessa College in 1970. They became close friends of mine and were very generous in sharing their New Mexico property. Neither ever seemed to experience a trace of frightening energy there. I did not either, those years back when Glenn and I camped there. Oh, but later I sure did! And so did our mutual friends, Patti and Joel Locke, who were also from Odessa.

While the Lockes were staying in the Furst/Burger cabin (with locked doors), Patti's purse mysteriously disappeared. Later during their stay, she saw a man wearing overalls in one of the bedrooms (again, the doors were locked). She said he was transparent, bending over a bed, and Patti could see right through him. He resembled Burger, who had died back in Odessa a short time before this apparition. The Lockes suffered no harm during their stay other than mental distress and the loss of a purse. But once they were back home, they resolved to never return there again. I think they have not, even after thirty-five years.

Some time around 1976 I took my young children, Billy and Sawndra, and our Irish setter, Cadmium Red, to this abode. It was late December, and it was New Years Eve. The first night of our stay we were cozied up by the fireplace when Cadmium Red suddenly bristled, bared her fangs, and began viciously barking. I was alarmed because some of the locals in the area were known to be Penitentes. Some were aggressive anti-Texan people and anti-hippie as well. There we were, both Texan and what might be considered to be hippie. At least we appeared to be the latter because we were driving a 1970 VW van with Texas license plates. In 1976 that was about as hippie looking as one could be. The various anti-hippie and anti-Texan signs I had seen did not add to my feeling of quietude. There were signs around the area stating *Texan Go Home!!!* and *Hippie Go Home!!!* They were big signs with bold lettering.

It was winter and bitter cold! It was less than ten degrees Fahrenheit. We had walked across the frozen river to the cabin because the snow and ice kept us from driving across. Then, the key Dr. Furst had given me would not open the locks on the doors! I went to each and every one outside and tried them all—several times. With freezing and numb fingers, I tried and tried to open the locks. We could not get in. The key simply would not work. It was dark and getting darker. The kids were freezing. I was freezing. I was about to panic. I do not remember precisely what I did, but somehow I jimmied a window and got into the cabin. Lord, it was cold inside that dark cabin, but at least there was electricity and there was a fireplace, so there was some hope for forthcoming warmth.

We got a fire going. God had saved us all! The fire was warm and glowing which was a graciously received relief from the bitter cold outside. We spread the bedrolls on the floor in front of the fireplace, thinking that there we would be safe and warm. We were safe and warm for a brief while. That is when Cadmium barked, bared her fangs, and bristled the hair on her back.

Since the snow was too deep for us to have driven up to the cabin, I had parked the van by the gate on the road across the river. This was fifty or sixty yards distant. I was frightened, and I did not want to alarm the kids. In a casual manner, I went outside with a flashlight and looked for tracks in the snow. I was holding the fireplace poker in my hand. There were no tracks, neither human nor animal, other than our own.

The cold was intense. My breath was white. I beamed the light across the field towards the van. A figure stood motionless beside it. My heart pounded! Quickly, I went back inside the cabin and removed a one hundred dollar bill and a credit card from my wallet. I placed both under a doily on the refrigerator and gathered sticks from the stash of firewood. I placed them strategically about the cabin, along with a small hatchet I found. I would have a club or weapon within quick reach no matter where I was. Through the night the dog raised her hackles and made low growling sounds. I pretended to sleep, but I did not.

It was a long, long night, and it passed without further incident. Daylight revealed no tracks around the cabin and none around the van; daylight also found us packing up and hauling out of that place! It remains a mystery to me who or what that ominous figure standing beside the van was.

Strangely enough, despite my vow to not do so again, I returned to the place. It was two or three years later, and it was again just after Christmas, again with my two children, and this time also with the object of my affection—my intended, my girlfriend, or whatever the proper term for her would be.

This experience was like a horror movie. It was cold and icy. Snow was on the ground. Everything seemed weird. Everything was weird. First of all, my girlfriend began acting incredibly strange and distant. I could not touch her or even kiss her. Every affectionate move I made was rejected. She would stare at the ceiling with very wide and very open eyes, almost as if she were in a state of catatonia. There was a foreboding and unsettling energy that seemed to saturate the entire premises. Although it was the dead of winter and the dark of night, flies appeared. They were large and fat. They had swollen green abdomens. They were blowflies. They swarmed the cabin by the hundreds, then by the thousands. We swatted them. We swept them into piles and into dustpans then threw them outside on the frozen, white, icy snow. They kept coming. We connected the vacuum cleaner and sucked them out of the air with the hose in a manner much as a fencer would wield a foil. They still kept coming. We fought them for two days then left to go back to Texas, where my lover bade me goodbye forever—leaving me to endlessly ponder the mystery of her sudden turn-off and chill.

Once more I had no intentions of ever returning to that cabin, but I did, and again it was several years later. I was with a friend by the name of Judy Sanders (AKA Sunny Sanders). We had been on extended and fascinating odysseys to old Indian ruins, desert places, and mountain streams. We were in the area of Las Vegas and were looking for a place to camp. Burger had died in 1977. Lovita, Burger's widow, and the Fursts had divided their property, and the Fursts had constructed another cabin, leaving the older one to Lovita.

We arrived in the summer twilight. It had been nearly a decade since I had been there, and I was a bit curious about how I would feel when returning to the site of such previous emotional distress and a place that had produced such negative energy. I was anxious. I was both fearful and apprehensive to peep into that old cabin—the place that had held such unrest and uncertainty for me a few years back—the place where the flies had swarmed and where Carole's heart had turned to ice. I approached it and was just about to step onto the porch when for some reason, some reason known only to God, I made an about face and went back to the van. Judy said nothing, but she had a strange look upon her countenance. I told her I wanted to camp somewhere else, and we headed towards Santa Fe. It was only then that I spoke of past adventures at the cabin, telling her the stories about Joel and

Patti, about me with the kids and Cadmium Red, and about the time
with the kids, my girlfriend, and the flies. As we drove through the
darkness, she confided that as I was about to step onto the porch, a bolt
of fear suddenly went through her. She had feared for my life. She was
paralyzed with terror. She was consumed with so much fright she could
not scream at me to warn me of the danger she was feeling. She sensed
that someone was about to slit my throat. We made it into Santa Fe and
camped at an RV park.

    The Gallinas River country is Penitente country. That is country
where the natives have little tolerance for anyone who is not of their
kith. That is country I have not been back to. That is country I stay away
from. That is country with an energy that beckons only to a certain
group, and I am not a member of that clan. That is country that for me
is a land of bad dreams. That is country that makes me feel as though:

> I've been riding forever
> In this land of bad dreams
> On a horse that's gone crazy
> He's white-eyed and mean
>
> He runs where he pleases
> He's impossible to reign
> He's taking me forever
> 'Cross these never-ending plains
>
> And he runs me by a river
> Flowing sorrow and tears
> With gushing springs of trouble
> And deep pools of despair
>
> He rides me through a forest
> Where the trees have no leaves
> Where the flowers smell like sulfur
> And fire is in the breeze
>
> Past rocks that are burning
> Where the sand smokes and fumes
> To a valley where the clouds are black

And blood is on the moon

Well it's been an eternity
Since I have seen a smile
Or had one single pleasure
Or rested for a while

This beast I'm on keeps running
Angry and mean
Lord please awaken me
From this never-ending dream

Lord please awaken me
From this land of bad dreams

I've been riding forever
In this land of bad dreams
I've been riding forever
Riding forever ∼

    I love New Mexico, but for me that area of the state is a place
of bad dreams. It is in vivid contrast to the euphoria that most of the
other parts of the state produce for me. For me it is a place of negative
energy, a place from which I stay away. But even as I write, something
stirs within my mind, and I think what would it be like now? Should I
go back and find out? I wonder.

XVIII.

THE LOWER PECOS RIVER

BY FAR, THE PLACE OF MYSTERY, POWER, ENERGY, and intrigue that has been the most significant of all to me is the Lower Pecos River area of Texas. The Pecos River could have obtained its name from the conquistadores as they explored its upper regions in the *Sangre de Cristo* Mountain Range of northeastern New Mexico. There, the stream is crystal clear, full of trout, and it splashes and laughs over incredibly motley stones. This could have led the Spaniards to call it *pecoso*, a word meaning freckled. Later, the name supposedly became

MILES CANYON, SHOWING EAGLE CAVE EAST OF PECOS RIVER. A WORLD HEAVYWEIGHT PRIZEFIGHT WAS STAGED IN THE MIDDLE OF THE RIO GRANDE AT MILES CANYON IN 1896.

PLACES OF MYSTERY, POWER & ENERGY

contracted into the anglicized word, "Pecos." The word Pecos could also have come from the Latin word *pecus,* which means a single head of cattle. It could also have come from the Spanish verb *pecar,* which means to sin or to do wrong. Whatever the word might mean to other cultures or in other languages, to me it means an exciting river and an area of fascinating archaeology. To me, it means energy that founded an art career.

This wonderful river begins as a spring, or as a series of springs, in New Mexico's Truchas Wilderness. It flows across that state, then across Texas making a confluence with the Rio Grande River near Langtry, that famous place on the Texas/Mexico border where the notorious Judge Roy Bean hung out and hanged out. It is some seventy miles west of Del Rio, just across the river from Ciudad Acuna, where the legendary Wolf Man Jack voiced his border radio broadcasts over North America, across Canada, and probably to the North Pole.

I have stated that I have always had an involvement with the Land. I came from the land, must return to the Land. I was floating the Lower Pecos River, floating it and photographically documenting the lower portion of it. Since that time in 1979, my involvement has been to paint and sculpt elements from that river and from the nearby section of the Middle Rio Grande.

In the spring of 1979, Wallace Bosse, Bill Murchison, and I floated two canoes down this wonderful and remote ribbon of water and life. We put in at the Pandale Crossing and paddled to Mexico, a distance that we calculated to be 66 miles. This happened during the last few days of May and the first few days of June. We were creating a photographic essay of this area for *Outside Magazine,* which was then based on the West Coast. On this adventure we encountered inundating rains and unbelievable lightning storms. It was as if the oceans were in the sky secured by some gargantuan zipper and that some Force had then unzipped the zipper and released those vast oceans onto the Chihuahua Desert allowing them to fall upon and around three small human beings—three small creatures who were somewhere in the Trans Pecos wilderness.

For brief instants the earth was strobe-lighted, and the thunder was deafening. For a fraction of a second, we could see as if it were high noon, then the illumination would collapse and the blackness would compress all existence into the confines of the tiny cave in which we had huddled for safety and refuge. The proximity of this cave to where we had been near sundown was no accident. We had spotted it from a mile up river, and due to the ominous sky, we had made it our contingency.

Our surroundings became blacker than a charcoal drawing on a lignite wall. Suddenly, there was a tremendous roar—like that of a freight train. We used our flashlights to watch a high wall of muddy, rolling water carry rocks and sticks and whatever else was in its path down a side canyon and dump it into the Pecos. To speak in laconic terms, it was "awesome!" This was not the only storm to hit us on this trip, and this tiny cave was not the only one that served as our shelter. What a season for a canoe trip! We could not have timed it worse. Of course we could have no way of knowing then that we could not have timed it better, at least as it turned out for me.

These rock shelters were rich in pictorial art, and at the time, even though I was spellbound by it, I had no concept of its marvelous antiquity. There were vast amounts of cultural debris strewn about the floors. Some of this debris had been swept from the shelters in ancient times. It was piled into great heaps on the slopes in front of the caves. This was 2,000 year-old garbage at the surface level, and at the bottoms of these trash piles were leavings from 12,000 years in the past. This was mere trash to the ancients. To modern man it is treasure. Mostly it is burned rock, and within those mounds of it are flint artifacts and artifacts of other materials. There are *manos* of stone and stone *metates*, remnants of *sotol* leaf weavings, shells, painted pebbles, and various tools of bone and deer antlers. Additionally, there are coprolites and human burials. We looted none of it.

There were two caves we took for refuge on that trip. The second cave had a deep layer of dust upon its floor, and into this centuries old accumulation, I made an excavation. With a stick, I dug a very short way into the dust and debris on the floor. I uncovered a metate (grinding stone) with a mano (pestle) still on top in the cavity of the metate. I photographed these and then carefully covered the hole. When we left the cave the following morning, we cut small bushes from the banks of the Pecos below. We bundled them to sweep clean our traffic marks, each and every footprint we had made. Even the ashes from our fire we dumped and then swept the area clean. We did no harm, for the bushes we cut would grow again in a short time.

It is paradoxical to me that private individuals who dig and loot these ancient dwellings are referred to as vandals by degreed archaeologists, and yet these degreed scholars—mostly university professors—themselves loot the shelters, classify the artifacts, and store them in dark basements out of public view. I was told by a very reliable source, a person with a doctorate in archaeology, that in the 1930s the Smithsonian exhumed some sixty-five ancient burials along the Lower Pecos River and the Middle Rio Grande River, crated those human remains, shipped them to Washington, and they are still there, still in crates. This person told me the crates have not been opened since. I think there is karma about such legalized piracy and theft. Perhaps our ancestors will come to haunt those involved. The energy of those ancient spirits will be reckoned with some day.

After we had taken shelter in these caves, I was on fire with inspiration and spent the next seven years studying and developing a style that would express my feelings and my emotions about what I had experienced. At least I attempted to express these. Our greatest attempts in such artistic renderings are but attempts to express what we deeply feel. The Lower Pecos forever changed my thinking, my art, my career, and probably even who I am or who I came to be. What a journey it was! It could not have been timed better! What an odyssey it still is! I am grateful for the experience. I still feast upon the magic, mystery, power, and energy of the Land. I still feast upon being a part of these and in some way being a part of those ancient artists and bygone peoples who are my teachers and my mentors. Those mostly isolated humans of the Lower Pecos River and the Middle Rio Grande River— that territory that lies on the border dividing what is now Texas and Mexico—vanished forever, leaving us to wonder from whence they came and where they went. What a fascinating mystery they are, having left the energy of their four thousand year old painted murals upon the walls of the rock shelters.

PAINTINGS ON THE WALL OF A CAVE IN WHICH WE
TOOK SHELTER. THE LONG, LINEAR PAINTING IS
SOME 20 FEET IN LENGTH, SURROUNDED BY MANY
ANTRHOPOMORPHIC RENDERINGS.

I return to the area now and then, just to soak in the magic, just to be there, to muse and to ponder, and to gain inspiration. I am a creature of the desert. I must return to the desert.

To view a marvelous rock shelter and some of the ancients' paintings that are upon its wall, search the Internet for Seminole Canyon State Park Comstock, Texas. Additionally, there is information about the prehistoric peoples who inhabited the area. Remember, when you hear some tour guide state interpretations of this ancient art, *caveat lector!* By all means, *caveat lector!*

LEFT: *"SYMBOL"* STERLING SILVER PENDANT AND THIS PAGE, *"SYMBOL"* BRONZE WALL HANGING.

XIX.
THE TUNNEL OF LIGHT

IT WAS A SCORCHING SUMMER DAY in Brewster County, Texas. We were on what was then known as the Chambers Ranch, far to the west of the Big Bend. This is a vast and rugged wilderness. From where we were, the nearest outpost was over three hours away and, unfortunately, another two hours beyond that to the closest beer store. Sam Baker, Theresa Chambers, and I were standing before a small rock overhang. It was an overhang in a prodigious boulder. It was June 26, 1996. The plus 100-degree afternoon was bone dry, and the sun beating down upon us made the thought of a cold beer much more than inviting.

Upon the wall of this shelter were pictographs, mostly handprints, and alongside these were the only prehistoric footprints any of us had seen. The only differences in the sights we perceived around us and the sights those ancient artists probably perceived back in other eons were our modern apparel, my Chevrolet Suburban in the distance, and above us one very high, thin jet airliner vapor trail. From where we were, it was 80 miles in a straight line to anywhere, and getting to anywhere necessitated driving over the roughest winding road imaginable, making the drive much longer than the straight line distance.

I made a hike to the vehicle to get a camera. Fortunately, I remembered the Boy Scout motto and was prepared. I also had a cooler, ice, and beer in that vehicle. It was nectar! As we stood there upon the desert in front of the ancient paintings, Sam said, "Ten years ago today."

"What?" I asked.

"That's when I was blown up by the terrorists," he replied. What a horror story that is!

Sam had told me about the horrible Peruvian event that had been staged by The Shining Path, a violent South American terrorist group. The carnage was terrible. It maimed his cord-fingering hand so badly that he now plays left-handed guitar. The blast blew out his right eardrum. He had over sixty puncture wounds, some of them cutting arteries. He was at death's door. A United States Air Force plane evacuated Sam and some others, flying them from Lima to Brooks Air Force Base in San Antonio, Texas. There the medics wanted to amputate his legs. Sam was refractory! He would not allow it! Sam had told me about his journey through the tunnel of light, that near death experience that has been reported around the earth. A few months earlier, I had written the following in one of my journals:

THE TUNNEL OF LIGHT

I have heard about it
I have read about it.
I have a friend who has traveled through it,
Or, at least, has seen it.
He was blown up and maimed in Lima,
On a Peruvian train
By a terrorist's bomb.

He saw the Tunnel–
The Tunnel of Light.

Even with our modern skills of articulation
The best descriptions seem clumsy.
With paper, pens, canvas, brushes, and paints
We still cannot convincingly render it
Nor describe it.

I ask you,
How would you draw a tunnel?

How could the Ancients have possibly drawn it?
Painted it?

They had a poverty of implements
Compared to ours.
They had no written language,
So, how could their concepts of it
Be passed down to us
Other than by this simple
Petroglyphic and pictographic diagram?

The Tunnel of Light.

    The painting I referred to above in my notes was a desert landscape. At the point when I would have considered it complete and then signed it, I painted a spiral over the entire painting. Then I thought it was probably finished, and I signed it. I had been thinking about this

image for a long time and what it might symbolize. Then I wrote THE
TUNNEL OF LIGHT, that writing above, on the back of the canvas
and leaned it against a wall in my studio.

Not long afterward, by happenstance perhaps, Sam Baker came
by my studio. When he saw the painting, he became almost catatonic.
I left him alone for a while, and when I returned, he instantly said,
"Worrell, that's the tunnel of light. I've been there. You've been there too
or you could not have painted it." Then I showed him the writing, and
we both got goose bumps.

Sam stayed over that night. It was late in the evening, and I was
working on a drawing that was to appear in the limited edition of my
first book, *Voices From the Caves – The Shamans Speak.* Sam was seated on
the couch, and I was at the easel sketching and listening to him play and
sing a Jesse Winchester song named "Songbird." Out through my hand
and the charcoal it held came SYMBOL, my personal favorite of all my
creations, and by far the most popular. It combines two ancient symbols,
the spiral and the cross. Sam looked at it and exclaimed, "That is a
powerful image." It was and is a powerful image. It shows up in many
places, such as in videos, on talk shows, and in commercials. It is always
a fun thing for me when I am watching some music video or some talk
show and I see famous personalities wearing SYMBOL.

In 2002 Sam and I were playing a gig at The Pier on Lake Austin
with Stephanie Urbina Jones. When I introduced him, I made mention
of his left-handed guitar, his puncture wounds, and the dynamite charge
planted in the train over his head. He took the stage and said, "Seventeen
years ago today." I had no idea that it was June 26. A similar incident
happened on the 19th anniversary. Some energies do not cease.

Sam Baker produced a CD in 2004. It is entitled *Mercy.* Part of
it deals with the Peruvian event. It is a wonderful production and has
contributed to Sam Baker becoming a major star in Europe! It can be
located on the Internet. Visit sambakermusic.com or search *Mercy* by
Sam Baker. You will hear some incredible music on this recording. His
next CD is entitled *Pretty World,* and his third is labeled *Cotton.*

Energy!

XX.
INVISIBLE
FORCES

SOME BELIEVE SPIRITS FLOAT around in the sky, in heaven, or in the ethos. Some believe inhabiting spirits hang around places within the landscape and not just float around in the air or in the sky. Some believe there are spirits that occupy dwellings, buildings, and other structures. There may be and there may not be. The considerations are intriguing. No one can prove there are not spirits or ghosts because it cannot be proven that anyone has not seen them. If I see a presence—a spirit—a ghost, and I know I saw it with my very own eyes, I still might not be able to convince another person that the epiphany was genuine, and it could be argued with credibility that the event was a hallucination or some figment of my imagination. It could also be argued that I was simply lying. Most interrogators would consider that I was just creating images in my mind; I was dreaming, or I lacked the ability to distinguish what is real from elements of fantasy.

I find it interesting that one of the greatest of all causes for war, dispute, and conflict has centered around invisible forces. There is argument regarding Moses and the burning bush and about the issuing of the Ten Commandments, those allegedly given to Moses by God on Mount Sinai. There are those who believe God gave them to Charlton Heston, too, one of the many myths Hollywood has fostered. It has also been questioned whether the golden plates that an angel allegedly directed Joseph Smith to find is true. It has been true regarding the resurrection and epiphany of the risen Christ. It has been true regarding the alleged revelations given to the illiterate sheepherder, Mohammad. Some maintain that he could not have possibly monitored or even proofread the supposed dictations he would have had to give to his scribes in order to produce the Koran. It follows there is great controversy over just how the Koran (or Quran) was written and who authored it. It holds true to this day regarding the rantings and ravings of self-appointed gurus, prophets, and preachers, whose exhortations seem mostly to be, "Do as I say, not as I do."

It is perhaps impossible to prove the existence of spirits because they are intangible. However, so are radio waves. If radio receivers and transmitters were not such ubiquitous inventions, I might not be able to convince you that they are real at all. To get a grasp on how frustrating it might be to convince someone of the reality of invisible forces or existences, imagine how it might be if you could travel back in time to the 1860s, and you could take both radio transmitters and receivers with you. Suppose then that you set transmitters up in Springfield, Illinois, Washington, D.C., and in other towns between. You would have disc jockeys, CDs, CD players, transistor radios, newscasters, and everything else that goes along with modern-day radio broadcasting. Then you present President Abraham Lincoln with a small solid-state radio receiver. Imagine your conversation with the president.

"What is this?" asks Abe.

"It is a radio," you tell him.

"A what?"

"A radio."

"A radio? What does it do?" and you begin to try to explain.

Create the ensuing conversation for yourself and how you might explain this little magic box to Honest Abe. Consider how his doubts and disbelief would rise as you told him what this magic little device would do. Consider how his doubts would then evaporate as you had him turn on the power. He would still be in doubt until you taught him the device needs to be "tuned in" to receive a particular broadcast from a particular station. It would still require independent investigation and exploration on his part as he rode the rails from Springfield to Washington a few times, tuning in to the news and to the music fading in and out from the different stations. He would finally conclude for himself you were not lying about radio waves, and he would realize the necessity of being "tuned in." Being tuned in is also a necessity for receiving certain other energies—such as metaphysical energies. One might think the existence of cell phones, smart phones, the Internet, and other digital technology would make us a bit more open to other possibilities.

As I would not have been lying to Lincoln about radio waves, I am not lying about ghosts either. I have spoken to them. There follows a true story.

In 1982 or 1983, Patti Shadburn wanted to camp by the Llano River at New Art. That was agreeable with me, and Sunny Sanders and I were already set up there, just a few dozen yards from where Patti elected to pitch her tent. There was a trail that led from the campground through a brushy thicket and up a rise to a very fine and classy outhouse with a shed in close proximity. It was an A-frame outhouse, complete with a door, a draw curtain, and a picture of Will Rogers at his mailbox. That was one of the few fineries out here in those days, along with that shed which we called "The Hilton."

It was a dark, dark night. Nature called. Patti answered. Patti did not answer for long! She sprinted back to the campground, and as she babbled and panted, we could see—even in the summer night's darkness—that she was pale with fright. Not only that, she was chilled with shock. When she was finally able to talk, she told us that as she was walking towards the facilities, she had a vision of some presence coming up behind her, slitting her throat, and ripping out her heart. It was an ugly vision and she was a shaken woman! She pulled up her tent and moved it next to us. This got Sunny "started," and for a considerable amount of time, the two exchanged stories of mutual horrors and common fears that focused upon ghosts and evil spirits. They seemed to resemble two metronomes, tick-tick-ticking away at those supernatural tales. I sat and listened in amazement to their nonsense, irritated by the disruption of such a quiet and peaceful night.

Not long afterward, I was to learn there had been others who had experienced feelings of uneasiness and dread on that trail to the outhouse and the shed. Jackie Hunt, a physician friend, experienced a quiet chill on a hot July afternoon. Some "cold, clammy wind," she said, along with a strange swarm of blowflies. It was not explainable and was not reasonable, but she said it happened and Jackie was not one prone to fabrications. I do not remember the details of some of the other stories. All of them made me irritated, and I brushed them aside. They did make me wonder a bit, though, and that exacerbated my irritability kindled by such nonsense. More than that, my wonderings increased as I listened to and reviewed their stories. I, too, experienced that chill, not knowing about Patti's or Jackie's experience.

I attempted to have an open mind. I try to do that sometimes—unless I know somebody is wrong, totally misguided, and in total diametric opposition to my opinions. After all, I cannot see electricity, but I have little doubt about its existence. I can't see radio signals either, but I hear the voices of my many wonderful Nashville friends over speakers in my vehicle. I look up at night through the blackness of the sky and know that there is sunlight streaking past; it is above the dark side of this planet. It is right before my eyes, even though I cannot see it. I know it is there for it causes the moon and the planets to glow, but I can't see it until it is reflected off something: Mars, Venus, the Moon, or my retinas. But its non-visibility does not create disbelief for me about its presence.

So I got to thinking I had best ponder this ghost, this Spirit thing. I did, and I found that, as with all metaphysical quests, the road to discovery was a lonesome journey. Some things can only be discovered privately. I did ask questions, though, and lots of them. I blatantly asked people if they believed in ghosts. "Ask and it shall be given to you," it is written. Was I ever overwhelmed—with ghost stories!

As I write these words, I will tell you I cannot remember one person denying the existence of Spirits without some reservation or some qualification. It seemed I was the only one with a closed mind. Not everyone had witnessed some presence or some revelation, but many had, and quite a few gave fascinating accounts that raised the hackles on the back of my neck. I began to wonder who these Spirits are and where they came from. Why are they here, if in fact they are here?

A few hundred yards west of New Art is an old stone house. I call it a "ruin," for lack of a better term. It dates back to the late 1840s or the early 1850s and was erected by German settlers. It was long ago abandoned, and afterward some of the later arrivals into the area tore away many of the wonderfully hewn and handcrafted stones to build other structures, just as they did with Fort Mason a few miles northwest. Etched into the plaster on one of the walls is an account that some quasi-literate person recorded with backward "S's," reversed "N's," and spelling worse than even my own:

> This room hs gosts. You can her
> them. You cant stop them. Red men
> cam over walls killed 2 wives and 5 girls—

This inscription is difficult to read now, and it becomes more weathered and eroded with each passing year, but it is serious graffiti. It is lore handed and re-handed down. In a clumsy yet charming manner, this is some unknown author's attempt to link us with the past and to record and preserve the account of an Indian raid or retaliation in the 1800s.

THE OLD RUIN ON LOWER WILLOW CREEK ROAD.

There are other stories about the place, too, like the heinous murder of a black girl after the Civil War (I always have difficulty considering that any war can be civil). There is absolutely no way to validate any of these tales, and of course, conversely, there is no way to dispute them either. And who but God knows the saddened and tormented spirits that dwell in the vicinity? What restless, wandering souls could these spirits be?

By 1984 Medium Cotton had been constructed, at least the first stage of it had been. It is now a rather plush, primitive guesthouse which was named as it is because I did not wish to be pretentious. In those days it had only electricity, a dirt floor, a telephone, and an outside water faucet. I lived in Medium Cotton during the six years I was constructing my house. I love it! I moved back into it a few years ago because it is such a fine and comfortable place. When I have guests, I am pleased to sometimes quarter them there, even though doing so necessitates my sleeping in the big house.

In those earlier years of New Art, I was hanging out in Medium Cotton when I realized this ghost thing had gotten a bit out of hand, and I had a lot of difficulty getting it out of my mind. My closest neighbor was a mile and a half distant, and the next closest lived about four miles away— both of them much too close for my comfort. There would not be more than three vehicles a week traveling the road that ran through my place. I didn't believe in ghosts, but sometimes I got a bit edgy living in such a remote place. Not too edgy, just a bit. Night birds made their sounds, coyotes called, and lonesome cattle and goats bawled. I could recognize these sounds, but now and then there was something strange, something that I could not quite put a handle on. That was what made me edgy, certainly not the solitude or the thoughts about ghosts.

About ten o'clock one midsummer night, I telephoned my brother from Medium Cotton. He was in Ohio. His name is John and he is a genius, or at least a prodigy. I regard him as the ultimate pragmatist, the epitome of the scientific mind. He was graduated from high school at age sixteen and was a graduate of the University of Texas at Austin at age nineteen. At age twenty-seven, he was a licensed physician in Texas, Colorado, and New Mexico, in addition to holding a Ph.D. in mathematics from UT Austin. While earning his doctorate, he started from scratch and in one month passed the examination for technical writing in French. I needed to talk with someone scientific about this ghost thing, so I called him.

I was on—what these days of digital saturation is termed—a "land line" with a rather short cord, and I was pacing back and forth on the dirt floor—my usual custom when talking on the telephone. (I once picked up a very fine flint projective point in Medium Cotton while doing this. It was knapped some five or six thousand years in the past.)

"Hey, man, let me ask you something," I stated to my brother. "Would you be afraid to walk from Medium Cotton, down to the River, and up to the shed and the outhouse all by yourself, without a flashlight on a dark night?"

There was a pause, followed by a stutter, and then at last a qualified reply. A reply, not an answer, but I pressed for the latter and got it. To my "Why?" he stated "There might be snakes or something."

Without a doubt there were snakes! Rattlers: big ones, too. I had encountered them at unexpected times and in unexpected places. The thought of diamondbacks is omnipresent in the Texas Hill Country along with scorpions and cacti. Nothing new. It was the thought of the "or something" that troubled me more. A bit of dread overshadowed me as I realized what I was compelled to do.

At this point I acknowledge my insanity. I must have been insane to do what I did! Believe me when I tell you it was dark. The stars were bright but there was no moon, and by then, after the conversation with my brother, it was midnight. I don't think I have ever had a short conversation with him. We have solved over half of the world's problems, but no one has ever really listened to our solutions. Without a light, without anything, I left the illuminated primitive coziness of Medium Cotton and headed for the River. I would be lying if I told you I was not apprehensive. There were crickets, katydids, the darkness, and me—by myself. Surely there must have been a few hidden reptiles also, with eyes watching my every step, with unique sensory pits sensing my

presence. From the campground, I went up the trail through the grove
of brush and trees to the shed, and there I stood on the deck. The hinges
creaked as I opened the door and began speaking.

There I was, in the middle of a dark night talking to
something—or some things I did not even believe in. "Who are you?
What's going on? What is this all about? Are you troubled? Sad?
Anguished? Why? Why do you trouble my guests? No one here wishes
you ill. I wish you peace. Abide here in peace and harmony and good
will, but do not frighten my guests, damn it! Do not frighten my guests!
Please be here in peace. No one wishes you harm. Do us no harm.
Whoever you are, peace!"

The dread evaporated, and I walked back to the River and up to
Medium Cotton, fearing nothing, fearing nothing living or dead. I did
not mention to anyone what I had done for a long, long time. But I'll
tell you one thing, after that I heard no more complaints or stories about
ghostly presences at New Art.

There is a plot of land called "Lower Willow Cemetery" about
a mile east of New Art. In it are the graves of many early settlers. It
has crossed my mind to wonder if these Spirits come from there. I also
wonder if they come from the old house west of me. Sunny Sanders
owned these ruins and was terrified by them after sundown. Terrified is
not adequate to describe her fears. So on another dark night, probably a
time before my insane nocturnal odyssey, I took her there. In the room
with the "historical graffiti," I kicked back the weeds from the floor with
my boot heels and then built a small fire out of mesquite. We kept it
kindled for a couple of hours as we sat on the bare earthen floor making,
or attempting to make, peace with whatever and whomever might be
the spirits sojourning through or dwelling therein.

I do admit I have had my own dread about that place, too,
even after Sunny and I sat there that evening. I remember passing by it
another time on a late night while riding my mountain trail bike, when
there was just the slightest sliver of a deep yellow moon. This gave just
enough light for me to define a large—a very large and quite stocky
rattlesnake stretched out just a few inches from where my wheels were
about to be.

That snake could not have given a damn less that I was there. In the dim moonlight I saw it look at me nonchalantly as I passed by, and I will bet that if there had been more light, I would have seen it flicking out its little black forked tongue. The rattler did not frighten me nearly as much as that dark and foreboding house did that was only a few yards away. I'm talking about thirty feet away. I could not allow my eyes to even start to drift in its direction as I rode past. Something told me to keep pedaling, hard, fast, and to not even glance at it, so that is precisely what I did—or did not do, believe me! I was like Lot getting the hell out of Sodom and Gomorrah! Silly, isn't it, for a person who (said he) does not believe in ghosts?

I kept my focus on the road and ground it out through the gravel, the rocks, and the sand. For over two miles, I pumped—and so did my heart—until I hit the friendly, lovely, beautiful blacktop of Highway 87. I could have kissed that sweet wonderful pavement!

But then there was reality. At that juncture I had two choices. Three, actually. I could sleep in the bar ditch with the fire ants, or I could turn right, go to Art, and then back to New Art from the east, a journey of sixteen miles—over dark dirt roads. Or, I could turn around and go back the way I came, over the same two-plus mile journey that went back past the ruins again.

Sometimes I hate decisions—like the decision to get some exercise and thus free myself of the guilt for not working out that day. That was why I was on that nocturnal ride. I turned around, but I had every bit as much (or perhaps even more) dread the second time than I did the first time, sane or insane as it might be. One thing I knew for certain: I wanted to be back at Medium Cotton, safe and secure, with a good book and a cold beer. I wanted to be back there with bugs flying around and lighting on me, making me tickle and itch. Maybe even a scorpion or two stinging me. I didn't care. Something, anything, to get my mind off that road, those ruins, and whatever or whomever were the unknowns or the ghosts that might be lurking there. It was silly, stupid, and insane, and of course, nothing happened except my dread. But dread is a demon. Dread is energy. Dread itself can be a very frightening experience, and for certain, it is a very real one. I think dread has killed

more people than experience could ever hope to count.

Now, I cannot tell you or anyone else what to think or what to believe about ghosts and/or spirits. I can only speak for myself in this matter, but I suspect what I think or speak applies to anyone—or everyone. I have concluded various things among my many missions on this odyssey of life; two of them are to make peace with living persons, even if I do not believe in them and to make peace with the spirits, whoever they may be, even if "I do not believe in them."

TO THE LEFT OF THIS DOOR IS WHERE THE
GRAFFITI IS SCRATCHED INTO THE PLASTER.
IT IS NOT VERY VISIBLE NOW.

XXI.

KELLER'S STORE

ABOUT TWO MILES WEST of the old ruin on Lower Willow Creek Road—that place where the graffiti about the Indian raid is on the wall—is Crockett Keller's place, known now as Keller's Store. This is where Sam Baker, Walt Wilkins, Spider Johnson, and I played musical benefits. That is, we played there until Crockett closed his restaurant/store. This place is now over 140 years in its antiquity. Crockett's great grandfather was born in one of the structures, the old blacksmith shop. Another of the old buildings was taken to Lubbock, Texas, 300 miles to the northwest. There, it was placed at the Texas Tech Ranch Heritage Center. The house in which Crockett and his wife, Dianna, reside looks like part of an old movie set. I asked Crockett if he had ever had any indication there might be spirits about the place.

Crockett parried the question with a tale. He told me about an Indian raid that occurred in the 1800s, and the story was filled with fascinating details, including one about his finding a lance point in the field near the site of the stone structure that was moved to Lubbock. The lance point was dropped by an Indian brave who was thwarted in his attempts to rout the settlers from the dwelling. These were Keller's ancestors from Germany. Then he added he had not seen spirits or ghosts, but he has felt presences of some sorts. He stated he had even talked with them. "I talk to them in German," he added.

German immigrants settled Mason County. Are spirits confined to understandings only in their earthly native tongues? Does God understand English or only Hebrew? If God does not speak English, I am in a real mess. So are a lot of others like Jimmy Bakker, Jessie Jackson, Jimmy Swaggart, Pat Robertson, Jeremiah Wright, and a lot more. Pat is in enough trouble even if God does understand English as well as He understands Hebrew. And so is the alleged "reverend," Mr. Wright, who believes he uses scriptures to justify his breaking at least one of the Ten Commandments of the scriptures. "I say God damn America," he screamed from the pulpit. And thinking about it, I am presumptuous enough to assume some of the rest of those Gantry-like personalities are in trouble, too. Ah, but God is merciful.

Keller's Store is dark now—seven days a week. Perhaps energy dissipates. It seems to have either left that place or taken on a new form. I ride by and reminisce about the fun times we had there and how much the people loved being there, dining and listening to our music. Nothing lasts forever, does it?

RIGHT: DRAWING BY JIM EPPLER.

XXII.
HILL COUNTRY
MAGIC

THE HILL COUNTRY OF TEXAS IS A MAJESTIC PLACE. It is
a magic place, too. Many years ago the neighboring state of New Mexico
appropriately coined the slogan, "The Land of Enchantment." The same
could be said of the Texas Hill Country, for in that terrain there are live
oak trees that were already very large and stately when Columbus landed
in the New World. There are ancient burned rock midden mounds
where prehistoric people camped and cooked thousands of years in the
past. There are remnants of their artwork painted upon the cliffs and in
the rock shelters. There are miles and miles and miles of stone fences

that were laboriously erected by the early German settlers as long ago as 1855. The area abounds with wildlife. There are whitetail deer, Rio Grande turkeys, bobwhite quail, bald and golden eagles, and some 150 other species of birds. There are clear flowing streams and rivers, some with world-class fly-fishing, and there are wildflowers to be seen like nowhere else in North America. In the spring, there are certain areas where the hills literally turn blue with the vast coverings of bluebonnets, the state flower. The most highly populated bat caves in the world are in the Hill Country, and they draw thousands of spectators who come to view these flying mammals as they leave the caves in the evenings and return in the mornings.

With this abundance of flora and fauna, there are some undesirables, some aliens, too. Among them are fire ants. Fire ants have invaded the South and a lot of the rest of the country. Rumor has it they were first brought to America about 1935 in loads of timber imported from Argentina to Gulf Shores, Alabama. From there they have spread throughout the southern states and beyond. They have adapted oh so well! They are a threat to newborn animals and to quail and other ground-nesting birds. Their stings turn into festering sores, and if disturbed, they attack in swarms. Disturbing a fire ant mound causes one to wonder how one queen insect could possibly lay so many eggs.

Some have made light of their destructive traits, as did one former Texas agriculture commissioner. During a live television broadcast, he stated fire ants are not all that bad and people were overreacting to them. At that point the camera panned a field near Bastrop, Texas, that was literally covered with fire ant mounds. Before the camera, he stooped and stuck his hand into a mound. Almost immediately, he withdrew it, shaking it furiously and shouting, "Gawddamn!" He soon resigned as commissioner of agriculture. (There are rumors of other reasons why he resigned, too, like his infamous introduction to the memory of Martin Luther King at a convention of the NAACP in Austin. He certainly knew how to wreck a political career!)

There are a lot of cacti! Some pastures turn a rich yellow-gold in May as the prickly pears bloom. There is a small-bladed cholla that

the locals call "turkey pear." It has long thorns, and each of these is
covered with a thin sheath that often remains in flesh when the thorn is
removed.

There is a lot of stone in this area. One Texas Hill Country place
is named "Enchanted Rock." It is a huge and ancient bubble of granite
that covers some one square mile of surface area. It draws thousands
of tourists annually. In the Hill Country area, there is an abundance
of granite, limestone, sandstone, and flint. There are precious metals,
along with some of the finest topaz to be found anywhere. The largest
gem-quality topaz nugget in North America was found in Mason
County. The rocks and the vegetation are two of the reasons cowboys
wear boots and chaps. As in most, if not all, of the Southwest, there
are rattlesnakes—several species of them. There are also cottonmouths,
copperheads, and coral snakes.

Despite the thorns, snakes, scorpions, fire ants, and occasional
undesirable humans, this is the Hill Country that so many love. It was
here, on one bright, balmy spring morning, that Jim Eppler, David
Armistead, Spider Johnson, and I were walking the banks of North
Grape Creek, not far from the town of Fredericksburg. We came to
a beautiful waterfall that was cascading into a deep limpid pool. We
shucked our clothes and took a swim. Then we climbed upon the
limestone ledge from where the water spilled into the pool below. We
were like lizards basking in the warm spring sunshine when, without
one spoken word, the same impulse came upon the four of us. In unison,
we rose and started running. We had no clothes upon our bodies, and
we were wearing no footwear. We ran through the fields and the flowers,
over the pastures, and through the trees and bushes. We were sprinting,
not jogging. We did not tire! We ran and ran and ran, probably for well
over a mile, then returned to the pool and swam. It was a magical event.
Thirty-plus years later, we still marvel at the magic. We got not one
thorn! Not one grass burr! We bruised not one foot! We did not tire!
I cannot comprehend anyone of any age sprinting the distance we did
through such a terrain without tiring. I cannot imagine anyone running
as we did without clothes or shoes and not being cut and punctured by
rocks, mesquite, or cactus. To this day, we all agree we were under a spell
of some kind. We do not know from where it came, but it was upon us.

We were in a place of energy, mystery, magic, and power.

I often reflect upon that happening and never cease to be amazed by it. I would be insane to attempt to walk fifty yards—or any yards—in the Hill Country today without shoes upon my feet. I cannot imagine us running the way we ran without some injury of some kind. I muse that some memories are so very sweet, much like dreams of my youth. In those dreams I could fly. I really could.

RIGHT: SANTA FE CASITA.

XXIII.
A CASITA

NEW ART IS ON LOWER WILLOW CREEK ROAD, two and
a half miles from the U. S. Highway 87 Bridge. It is where Crockett
Keller speaks to the spirits in German. It is less than a mile from the old
ruins where the Indians raided, and where local lore claims a black girl
was murdered. It is one of those places of great and peaceful present day
energy, despite unrest of long ago. I feel this energy, and I have especially
felt it since that time when I performed the "nocturnal exorcism." My
guests feel it, or at least most of them express that they do. I could say I
own this place, but I do not because no one ever really owns anything.
A big mistake people often make is to assume they own things. Great

Spirit owns everything. Great Spirit simply lends things to us human beings and to other creatures. Here at New Art, as is true with "my" place in Santa Fe, I am simply a steward or a trustee who paid a certain sum of money in order to have such title— that is, to be able to control the places during part of my life time.

I call the place New Art because it is down a dirt road a ways from Art, Texas, which I refer to as "Regular Old Art." Since the 1800s, people have camped on the banks of the Llano River in front of what is now my home. They have picnicked there, had family reunions there, and have had Sunday "dinners on the ground" there. There are few who visit that do not feel some special energy at "my" place in Texas. I love this, am honored by this, and I hope this does not change.

I am what I refer to as bi-residential. I have a wonderful place in Santa Fe, New Mexico. Legally I own it, but again, I continually remind myself that I do not own anything. I am only a steward or a trustee of anything the courts and statutes have allowed me to state are mine. This Santa Fe place is a small historic adobe house that was once "owned" by Rosalea Murphy, founder of the famous Pink Adobe Restaurant. There is no doubt in my mind this is a place of special energy, and I have considered that energy might be added to energy: energy compounding energy, so to speak. In this case such energy was added by a gift from Ron and Karen Whitmore, owners of the Artisan Art Stores. In addition to being a chef, Rosalea was a painter, and I had longed for one of her works for quite a while. Because she was a friend of mine, I felt awkward about asking to purchase one of her paintings, and after she died her works were essentially no longer available.

One afternoon I had just pulled into Santa Fe from Texas when my cell phone rang. It was Ron at Artisan. He asked me to stop by the Canyon Road Store next time I was in Santa Fe because he and Karen had a gift for me. I had just driven the 600 miles from New Art to Santa Fe, and when he called fate had placed me within two blocks below the art store, so I simply pulled into the Artisan driveway.

"Karen and I have had this for you since we visited your house," Ron said as he handed me a package. I did not open the gift until I went home. That is just how I am sometimes. I become a bit embarrassed

when someone gives me something. When I did open it at the house on
Upper Canyon Road, I was floored! It was a Rosalea Murphy painting!
A few days later when I showed Ron and Karen where I hung it, Ron
said, "Some things just need to come back home." The painting came
back to the place where it was painted, and now my house has even
more energy than it previously had. I can feel it. And in my mind I can
still see Rosalea smiling.

I have various visitors and guests place their handprints upon
my walls in this Santa Fe casita. We place them around the fenestration
much as is commonly done with floral designs in the region. I have
guests do this with acrylic paint, and then I have the donors sign and
date them. There are handprints of everyday people and handprints
of famous people. Every time I collect another one, the energy within
the premises swells. There are handprints of famous musicians, famous
authors, famous artists, and friends who are famous to me.

Property changes possessors. Eventually it always does. The
federal government makes every effort to see that property is divided,
that it changes owners, that big land holdings are broken apart and
redistributed. That is the reason the government imposes the insidious
inheritance tax— "death tax," as it is called. The United States
government has a very subtle way of instituting socialism. Breaking up
the holdings of traditional ranches, farms, and properties of landowners
is just one of these ways. It might be a century in the future, or it might
be sooner than that, but things change. Someday I will no longer
be trustee of this casita. There will be a deed restriction that these
handprints cannot be removed and cannot be painted over—not ever! I
know, our society abounds with "trust busters." They can ruin the best-
laid plans of mice and men. They can bust them apart. Nevertheless, I
have attempted to be a good steward, and I have had trust tenets drawn
by an attorney. So during the process of paying (what I now think was a
shyster lawyer) big bucks to get my trusteeships in order, my friend Jay
Boy Adams and I wrote this song:

NEW ART, TEXAS STUDIO.

DON'T TELL NOBODY

The legislators get in seizure
Pass their greedy, greedy laws
Dig their hands in your pockets
Tie a noose around your paws

I

They tax you while you're living
Tax your children when you die
So if you want to keep the ranch
Don't let 'em know I'm not alive

Some things should be kept secret
They should never be revealed
Some things should not be spoken
Keep your lips tightly sealed

II

Once the word gets out
All kinds of mischief will arise
So don't tell nobody
Should I happen to die

Don't tell nobody
If I should die
The vultures will start circling
All over the sky

Chorus

Everything I have worked for
They will steal and divide
So don't tell nobody
Should I happen to die

I thought stealing was a crime
A Biblical sin
But politicians passed some laws
They make it legal for them

III
They will all go to Hell
Where they will forever fry
In the meantime don't let 'em know
When it comes my time to die

Jesus talked about the lawyers
And the tax collectors too
He said give to the government
What the government is due

IV
Give unto God
What God is due too
Jesus said they have no right
To take the ranch away from you

Repeat Chorus

I dreamed I had transcended
Met St. Peter at the gate
He said, "Boy you're here real early
I was hoping you'd be late

V
I trust you told nobody
You have left your earthly home
You better Get! Back! Down there boy
Before they find out you are gone

© *Worrell/Jay Boy Adams, 12/08/10, Waring, Texas*

XXIV.
RAVENS CAN LEARN TO TALK

THIS IS ANOTHER STORY about my casita in Santa Fe. My long time friend Wade Jarvis is about as colorful as a huge palette of paint. He is an unbending and unyielding personality. I have never seen him take any flack from anyone. He is a rugby player and is built like a Sherman Tank. I have seen him spin on a dime to confront someone who hurled an insult his way. He knows he has a hair-trigger temper and constantly works to ameliorate it, but the nature of his beast is hard to change, if change is even possible.

Wade can be a man of strong words. He can swipe the blue off his palette and color the air with it. He is as colorful with cussing as Jim Rabby is with paints. This often happens in half of an instant. It happens when some careless automobile driver with the HUA syndrome is stupid or negligent. It happens when some clerk at Home Depot is sassy with him. This happens when some implement or tool malfunctions or something goes amiss with a piece of equipment. It happens when the Dallas Cowboys fumble or miss a pass.

Wade was a roughneck, an oil well driller, and then became a building contractor. His work is precise and impeccable. It is as flawless as a human can make it. He helped me with my house at New Art, and not long ago, he was helping me modify the energy of my casita in Santa Fe.

While working on this project, I came to a conclusion that the Cliff Dwellers, the ones we refer to as the Anasazi, built structures to last for millenniums. The early day founders of Santa Fe built edifices to last for centuries. At some more recent point in time, builders in Santa Fe decided that nothing really needs to last more than fifty years, if even that long. It became obvious to me that this is what whoever built my back porch, deck, and roof thought. In fact, whoever built that roof probably thought it only needed to last until the next rain came because it would provide some shade until then.

Some of the rafters over this portal were not even nailed or pinned to the supporting ridge timber. There was no flashing against the wall of the house. The rafters were covered with some cheap, transparent, corrugated fiberglass that was broken easily and terminated over the middle of the supporting timber header. Of course, this caused the header to decay. Not only that, the entire structure was a trapezoid when it should have been a rectangle.

Thus the timbers were rotten, as were the *vigas* and *latias*. All of this seemed to give Wade a seizure of some sorts. There was a cloud of blue verbiage surrounding my quaint little adobe structure. My, my, how sound does travel up and down the canyon. I was amused at his cursing, and I was also a bit worried the neighbors would think it was coming from me. There are numerous ravens about the Upper Canyon area.

Wade would curse, and the ravens would answer. There were vile words. There were words that would make a sailor blush. There were words for which utterances my mother would have washed my mouth out with soap and water.

I love ravens. I love to hear them calling. I have incorporated them into my paintings and sculptures for many years. Fellow artist and friend Jim Eppler has made many bronze ravens, and I have some of them at my house in Santa Fe and at my studio at New Art.

There I stood with Wade upon my rooftop in Santa Fe, wondering if the neighbors thought I was screaming all those GDs, those MFs, those Ss, SoBs, and the uncountable damns. Then it suddenly dawned upon me that both ravens and magpies can learn to talk, and there is an abundance of both species up and down the canyon. So watch out now. Keep the women and children indoors, lest a flock of birds fly over Upper Canyon Road screaming GDSOB! MF! B! S! And Damn! Damn! Damn! Words carry a lot of energy, you know!

MONASTERY OF CHRIST
IN THE DESERT.

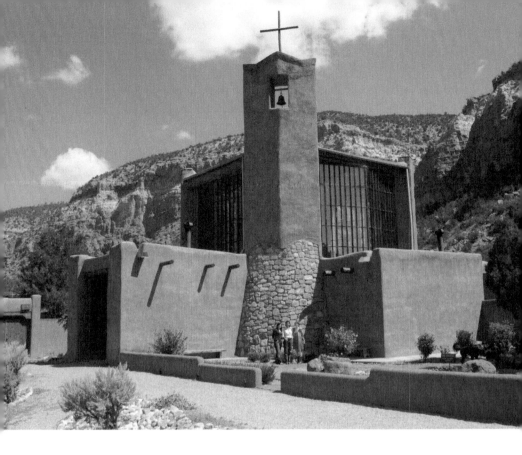

XXV.
THE MONASTERY

I SOMETIMES WONDER if the kind and gentle and benevolent spirits inhabiting a place can be driven away. I wonder if humans sometimes execute a sort of unconscious exorcism whereby they unwittingly do things that are offensive and repulsive to the good spirits. After all, people drive friends away, sometimes without intending to, without even knowing they do. People do things that change relationships. Why then could this not be true, that people can drive good spirits away?

One of my most favorite of all places is the Monastery of Christ in the Desert. I am Catholic, but I am not Roman Catholic. This confuses some people, but that is because they do not understand the term "Catholic" and do not make a distinction between Catholic and Roman Catholic.

I am politically protestant. I am protestant against most of the higher echelons and drones of institutionalized religion and education, and I am probably largely protestant against protestant denominations. Be this as it is, I have found this remote northwestern New Mexico Benedictine, Roman Catholic Monastery to be a place of great energy and power and even mystery. It has been and it is a place of great peace for me. I have had many wonderful and beautiful experiences there. I call it a church, but what I am referring to is actually a sanctuary or a chapel at the Monastery. It is situated close to the home of Georgia O'Keeffe and not too far from Ghost Ranch. As the foot walks, it is a long, hot—or cold, or just-right day's journey. It is about thirteen miles west of Highway 285. This is not too far, but it takes almost an hour to make the drive, unless it is raining or snowing; then, without four-wheel drive, walking may be faster.

Because the place is a monastery, the Brothers are bonded by Benedictine philosophies and are bonded by Jesus Christ. They are not, however, immune to conflicts, arguments, and disagreements. An interesting book about the history of Christ in the Desert, the Brothers, and various trials and tribulations that surround them is *Brothers of the Desert*, by Mari Grani.

The fundamental purpose of the Monastery, of course, is to deal with God. "God!" What a word. I mostly avoid using it because it has been so abused by so many. It has been abused by thoughtless souls who attach suffixes to it. It has been abused by charlatan souls who use it for their own power and gain. It has been avoided by fearful souls who shudder at the mention of it. Let me tell you, at one time there was no more fearing, despising, and rejecting a soul than I! I avoided God and anyone who claimed to have intimate contact with Him. But that is a much longer story and a part of the magic that comes from The Land of Enchantment.

Many a wandering soul has found the Monastery of Christ in the Desert. Many have discovered faith, belief, peace, and comfort there. Unusual things have happened there, too, such as the former prior (now abbot) assisting in the conversion of an atheist woman to Judaism. I would say that is a bit unusual—for a Roman Catholic Benedictine priest to lead someone to Judaism. Such a thing takes a lot of courage. Why? Because far too many people think God is going to be angry with them and do something terrible to them if they indulge or participate in any way in something that is outside the boundaries of their own religion. Such fear causes a lot of war! Such fear deprives us of many fine things. How well it would serve us to release ourselves from our prejudices, that bad, old energy. They fester. They generate fear. They bind us and confine us tighter than any prison could ever hold us, and I think many times they prevent us from absorbing the good energy, power, mystery, and intrigue that special places of magic offer.

There was a time when I was fearful of Roman Catholics and prejudicial towards them. I really desired to have nothing to do with them. Had I maintained that posture, I would have deprived myself of many a magical experience at this Monastery.

To get to this place, one must travel along banks of the Chama River near the places that Georgia O'Keeffe inhabited. The cliffs along this stream are grandiose, possessing colors pleasing to any artist's palette. The sanctuary, the chapel, the church, whatever the proper term should be, is a masterpiece of simplistic architecture. It is so wonderfully Southwestern one would be unlikely to surmise a man from Philadelphia designed it. This architect, George Nakashima, was not only a Japanese man from Philadelphia, he was also a Roman Catholic.

There is little doubt that this place has been a place of power and energy for many souls, including mine. But upon my most recent visit, something changed. For me, there was a different energy. I dread admitting it. I regret that I feel compelled to admit it, but something had changed. It is quite obvious that the grounds changed because for several years there was a large-scale building project. That project is now complete, or nearly so, if anything ever is complete. It has changed the appearance of the chapel, which in past times stood as a solitary feature—a Christian monument beautifully set apart from other structures—even though it was connected to the library and dining hall by a chamber in back. Now, it is also connected to a massive labyrinth of cells and rooms, a new dining hall, and even a new gift shop, which in the past also stood as a solitary edifice and was far, far removed from the proximity of the chapel.

At one time there were not even heaters or electric lamps inside the sanctuary. Then came the wood-burning stoves. Those certainly made life easier for the Brothers because temperatures can drop to ten degrees below zero and even colder than that. Following the stoves came solar collectors and a 12-volt lighting system, again making life easier for the Brothers. In prior times they read by candlelight. Then came a new idea followed by architectural renderings, the raising of finances, the groundbreaking, and finally a completed project: a sort of reconstruction. Along with these came the changing of the magic and mystery for many, including the family of the original architect, George Nakashima, who so thoughtfully and spiritually designed the chapel.

To me, and perhaps to some others, it has been a bit like painting a business suit over or around Warner Sallman's "Head of Christ." The simplistic beauty that once was there just seems to be gone, and it did not have to be this way. I know it did not, and I know there are many who could have designed the architecture so that the facilities would accommodate the monk's needs while preserving the beauty of the chapel. But I always keep in mind that this is their place. It is not mine.

I think those visiting this place for the first time will not be able to tune in to this, but for some of us there is a great loss. There is sadness involved because it simply did not have to be this way. The construction or remodeling was a product of convergent thought processes rather than of divergent ones. A different architect could have and possibly would have designed needed facilities without encroaching upon the sanctuary. Even a non-architect could have done it. I am arrogant I know, but even I could have done it, and I did, over and over and over in my mind. I kept designing and redesigning the structure even as my sister and I continued to donate to their cause.

Now the question for me is, did something change regarding the magic and power at the Monastery, or did something change within

me and within some of my friends? Has there been a change so that
I seem to no longer feel that wonderful old magic and delightfully
good energy that I once knew? Is it me, or is it the place? Do places of
power and energy sometimes lose their forces? This may happen just as
magnetic north has always been in a state of flux.

Many are the times I rejoice. Sometimes I cry.

XXVI.
ANCIENT & MODERN
ENERGIES

I AM BLESSED to experience and to have experienced the energies of many friends. I cherish both the experiences and the friends—each of them. Two of these are Mike and Leanne Wells. Mike is an artist. It is likely there is nothing he cannot make from steel. He was a helicopter pilot in Vietnam and honorably served our country during that confused and controversial conflict. Like every other veteran of that war, Mike met men who became his friends, and like many a veteran, Mike has stories. One of those who became Mike's friend was a support person of the U2 Spy Plane effort. The man's name is Eldon Swapp, which makes this story even more intriguing.

Eldon was sorely angered by the way the government was handling things in Vietnam. Eldon was so traumatized by the horrors of the experience that he located and purchased a very desolate and remote piece of property in the wilderness of Utah. He loaded everything up in a camper and moved there, far away from cities and far removed from congestion of civilization. After a time, he and his wife decided to build a home and terminate residing in the camper.

Eldon and his wife struck up a friendship with the chief (or perhaps the medicine man or shaman) of a nearby present-day Indian tribe, and the two would sometimes visit. During the construction process of his home, something happened that, although is not without precedence, is a bit apart from the ordinary. A lot of progress had been made in excavating and setting the forms for the concrete slab—the foundation for the new structure. Far along into this process, an ancient grave was uncovered. It predated the Cliff Dwellers, those often referred to as the Anasazi. It was very well preserved and was loaded with artifacts, namely pottery. Eldon was concerned. He did not want to commit sacrilege, and he wanted to maintain respect for the ancient dead. He had misgivings about covering the prehistoric site with concrete, so he called upon his friend, the nearby chief, for advice.

Eldon thought perhaps the remains should be exhumed and taken to the chief's reservation for re-interment. The chief was not in favor of this, telling Eldon that the remains of the woman were not of his tribe, and they were much more ancient than are his people.

The chief told him there was no harm in covering the grave with concrete because the woman's spirit was long gone from there, and the deceased woman would not mind his doing so. So Eldon decided to abide by the chief's wisdom and proceed with construction. But there was a problem. He just could not bring himself to pour a slab over the many items of fine ancient clay pottery that had been buried with her. He called the chief again and explained his consternation. The chief told him, "Indian always open to good trade."

And thus it came to pass that Eldon removed every pot from the grave. He purchased a brand new set of Revere Ware, and with that he replaced the items he took. Eldon Swapp swapped the Revere Ware for the ancient clay pottery! Then he continued on with the pouring of the slab.

Somewhere in the Spirit World, there is probably an ancient Indian woman who evokes great energy and great envy with her new culinary possessions.

XXVII.
THE ORCHID
GOWN

LISTEN to me boys, I've got a story for you
It is no fable, I swear that it's true
In New Mexico, past the valley of fire
Out in the wilderness, heart of my desire

I was riding for pleasure in the Mimbres Range
The summer sky was crystal blue, my horse had gone lame
I ain't accustomed to lying, and you know I'm not insane
But I've never seen nothing nearly this strange

There came a darkness in that summer sky
When across the canyon she caught my eye
From a piñon hill she was walking down
Some apparition in an orchid gown

I could see her form, view her loveliness
By the way the breeze blew through her dress
Burned in my memory in the desert light
As I approached her she vanished from my sight

There was nothing there but the blowing wind
Not one footprint where she had been
Just emptiness, and a mournful sound
And not one trace of that orchid gown

Boys, the desert has mysteries that I cannot explain
I was over the ridge 'fore I realized
There wasn't a trace of any kind
Not one trace of my horse being lame

It's been nearly thirty years, and I wonder still
Where is that woman on the piñon hill?
Her blond hair flowing as she was walking down
While the wind was blowing her orchid gown

Some apparition, some ghost I found
Some desert beauty in an orchid gown

These are lyrics that Jay Boy Adams and I wrote about an experience I had about twenty-five years ago in the Gila Wilderness of New Mexico. The song is a fable, of course, like many songs are, but the inspiration for the lyrics is the plain truth. I truly did see that beautiful woman in an orchid gown, and so did the person who was with me.

Just before New Years Day in 1998, I was riding in one of the most elegant tour buses ever created. It was designed and owned by Jay Adams, owner of Roadhouse Transportation and now also the owner of the Worrell Gallery in Santa Fe, New Mexico. Jay was taking me, along with his family, to Albuquerque to a Shania Twain concert. Jay Adam's Roadhouse Transportation has provided buses for some of the most famous of all musicians; Shania happened to be one of his clients. He constructs such elegant tour buses that he even put a Jacuzzi in her Roadhouse Coach!

We were out in the wilds of New Mexico crossing the area known as "The Valley of Fire." I could see, or at least I thought I could see, some mountains in the distance that I had once visited in the Gila Wilderness. This reminded me of an awesome experience I had there over fifteen years prior.

I had been with a friend, and we were traveling in an old beat up 1970 Volkswagen van. We had gone to Mogollon, to the Gila Cliff Dwellings, and were just taking our leisurely time prowling around the area. I was enthusiastic about doing some fly-fishing and catching a Gila trout, so we began driving on a dim dirt road alongside the Gila River, or as close to alongside it as we could.

We came upon an old Buffalo Soldier military fort— long, long ago abandoned. I spotted a side canyon to the east that appeared to make a confluence with the Gila River and thought there would likely be a fine hole of water there. It appeared to be about a half mile in the distance. I turned onto an even dimmer dirt road that seemed to lead in that direction. We came upon a flowing stream that crossed our passage. I did not know how deep it was, so I got out and waded across it to make certain we would not get stuck or stalled.

The sky, almost black, was ominous and the color of dark blue steel. It seemed it might come unzipped at any moment and pour oceans of water upon us. Having waded across the stream, I looked toward the canyon and saw a pickup parked in the distance. This gave me the assurance that we, too, would be able to make it over to that area in our vehicle. Volkswagen vans of that vintage will go almost anywhere, even places where some other vehicles might stall or get stuck. Thus I knew we could make it to where the pickup was parked. I got my binoculars and glassed the site. I was astounded! What I saw gave me chills.

The landscape was incredibly beautiful. There were rolling hills with piñon trees scattered upon them. In the distance the rolling landscape appeared so smooth it looked as if it had been manicured. The hills were a light golden amber color, contrasting against the dark and foreboding indigo sky behind them. A beautiful and shapely young woman was walking down the slope of one of these hills. I could see her plainly through the binoculars. She was striking, wearing a thin light-colored violet gown. The wind pressed it firmly against her lean rounded body. She had long flowing hair that resembled polished gold and which flowed out behind her in the breeze. She seemed to float down the slope more than to walk.

I handed the glasses to Sunny. She saw the vision also. I forgot about trout fishing. I could hardly wait to get to the spot. We crossed the stream and I gunned the engine. It was not so simple a task as it first appeared to be. There were ruts, gulleys, boulders, and other objects in our path, but we made it. When we finally arrived at the pickup, we found an elderly couple there. They seemed to be simple and plain folks dressed in denim clothing. They were sitting on campstools and drinking coffee and tea. I guessed them to be in their seventies. They were alone, or so they stated. We visited pleasantly for a while, talking about the abandoned fort, about Indian pottery and artifacts, about where they lived over in Hillsboro, and about the coincidences of knowing people in common. We talked until the sky turned even darker and the thunder grew louder. Then precipitation commenced, and I became fretful that the rain and resulting swollen stream would strand us. Sunny and I departed.

Down the road an hour or so later, it was quite sunshiny and beautiful. I was photographing an abandoned church as we progressed towards the village of Magdalena. Suddenly Sunny gasped, "The girl in the gown! What happened to her? Where was she?" I was amazed and flabbergasted that we both had forgotten about her. I was stunned by this, and Sunny was convinced we had been placed under a spell so we would not remember to inquire about her.

I know I will never forget the vision of that beautiful and shapely ghostly form that floated down a piñon hill in an orchid gown.

It was and still is a haunting image, wildly vivid against the dark blue-black sky of an impending New Mexico storm. It is etched in my memory. I think someday I may return to the place just to view the sky, the desert, and an empty hill with piñon and sage growing on the slopes. I may return there just to hear the wind blow, to be alone, to wonder, and to perhaps catch another glimpse of that beautiful figure in an orchid gown.

XXVIII.
APRIL DANCE

THERE IS JUST SOMETHING ABOUT TEXAS that produces magic, mystery, energy, and power. We get a lot of flack for talking about it, but it is true. It is true of other states, too, but Texans just seem to talk about it more than other people do. It was Friday, the twentieth day of the fourth month, 2001. I was a guest of Dr. D.J. Sibley and his wife Jane. It was the pre-opening party of the new Bob Bullock Texas History Museum in Austin. The edifice was magnificent, and it was packed with people. Exotic food was in abundance, along with an open bar and music by Rick Trevino, a rising young country music star.

This museum is alive and throbbing with the history and energy of Texas: Stephen Austin, Sam Houston, Bowie, Travis, Bonham, and the other heroes of the Alamo. It holds a rich accounting of political figures such as Lyndon Johnson, John Nance Garner, and others.

This was a notable and highly attended event; thus, it was no surprise that many of the attendees were beautiful Texas women, one of whom approached me with a warm, friendly greeting. The hard drive began spinning as my mind went on search in vain attempts to recall her name and from where or how I knew her. So I simply made my confession.

"I'm Temple!" she said. "Remember? I used to work for you!"

I faked a little embarrassment and replied, "Well, you were always pretty but never quite like now," and that was spoken in earnest.

Temple did work for me, for a short while, but her passion was music and not polishing, packaging, and shipping bronze sculptures. She now has a career as a singer and songwriter and is enjoying success performing in Holland. During our casual chatting, she informed me that my dear friend Kristen Nagel was at this party, somewhere in the building. It was Kristen who had first introduced me to Temple. As Rick Trevino began playing, Kristen entered the spacious rotunda lobby. She spotted me and asked me to dance. What a pleasure it was, dancing with those beautiful women.

Kristen and Temple were at this function with another beautiful woman, a Texan of French descent. Veronique caught my eye instantly. In fact, she caught both of them, and then I caught my breath. She was a gazelle with soft olive skin, flowing dark hair, and deep, dazzling eyes. She had a soft, charming smile and was wearing an exotic strapless white gown that very efficiently revealed her feminine beauty.

I was quite attracted to her, but there I stood, shackled and cuffed by the conventions of our culture; thus, all I could do that was socially acceptable was gaze upon her with admiration. My thoughts were not obscene or crude. They were thoughts that so often happen with creative people. In an instant—in a heartbeat—creative minds can compose a mental novel where they find true love and romance that endures till "death do us part." The problem with this is that, once the novel has been created, the characters seldom play their roles as written!

Kristen and I danced and then we danced again. Too soon, it was time for me to leave. The Sibleys were weary, and I had another engagement for a late dinner. Just prior to our exodus, Kristen said, "I know it is late and you have to leave, but first would you dance one time with my friend? She would really like to dance with you." I took Veronique by the hand and eagerly led her to the dance floor. I would be allowed to hold that beautiful body after all.

As we stepped upon the floor for "San Antonio Rose," she whispered, "I need your help. Please watch my dress so I will not be embarrassed if it slips down. I had a double mastectomy a month ago, and I have no feeling in my breasts." I acknowledged that I would do this with pleasure. I held her and we danced. We two-stepped and we swung. She moved so very gracefully it reminded me of how the softly blowing wind bends and stirs the cottonwoods and gently ripples the waters. The song ended, and that crowd of Texans applauded Rick Trevino for "San Antonio Rose," an incredibly famous tune written by the late Bob Wills. "Please clap for me," she smiled and said. "I can dance and I can spin, but my pectorals are too sore to clap." I did, and this beautiful lady and I danced again.

Though I am a gentleman and would never wish her the slightest embarrassment, I nevertheless had that sly naughty desire to see her dress slip and unveil the beauty of her breasts and the masterful art of an incredibly skilled surgeon. I am an artist, after all! I realized that a mastectomy, even a double mastectomy, is not the end of the world, not the end of sensuality, sexuality, or desire for a woman or for a man. It is not the end of many things, but it might be the beginning of a new and beautiful dance of life.

As she stood before me, her beauty metamorphosed even more. Again, I perceived her smile and gazed into those alluring eyes. There was a bright sparkling light coming from them, and in it I caught a glimpse of courage, determination, self-confidence, strength, faith, and hope. I caught a glimpse of a marvelous woman who, despite her physical discomfort, chose to place adventure over self-pity. I perceived a spirit who chose to go to a party rather than sit at home. I looked into those eyes, and there was no doubt that this woman knows she is in control of her own destiny.

We bade each other good night, and I left to meet other friends. Perhaps some day we will dance again. If not, I have no doubt that Veronique will be dancing with some lucky man who will be as enchanted, mesmerized, and intoxicated by both her physical beauty and her inward beauty as I am.

It was a wonderful evening, that April dance evening. There is just something about Texas that produces magic, mystery, power, and energy.

Veronique's husband had left her. He left her with a daughter in college and a son in high school. He left her with no insurance, no job, and in a physical condition too weak to practice her profession of horse massage therapy. He also left her with hospital and surgical bills. I am a bit embarrassed to write this, but I am doing it anyway due to spiritual and philosophical considerations.

I suggested to two of Veronique's close friends that they approach the surgeon and tell him I would trade art for her debt to him. They would not do it. Veronique would not either. Perhaps I sort of knew why Veronique would not; I did not understand why her friends would not.

So I sent a letter to her surgeon, explaining how awkward it was for me to write, and suggested he open my web site and contact any of our gallery affiliates to verify the monetary value of my art. I told him if he were interested, I would gladly create a painting for him. A few days later he called. He said he and his wife, Judy, would be very interested in making the trade. They drove from Austin to my studio in Art, Texas, to see some of my work, and we made the deal. Judy told me they had wanted my work since seeing it in Santa Fe ten years prior. I then had a revelation that skepticism is a demon that slams many doors of opportunity.

Having no desire to go on welfare, Veronique founded Hearts &

Hooves, a nonprofit organization that rescues animals, mainly miniature horses. The animals are housebroken and taken to hospitals, Hospice centers, Ronald McDonald Houses, and the like to visit, cheer, and comfort the sick and the elderly. The organization has grown and now has sub-chapters. Our gallery affiliate in Tubac, Arizona, is an affiliate thanks to Kim Roseman, the owner. Veronique and Hearts & Hooves have appeared on television shows, including *The Today Show*, and have been featured in publications. To request a visit from this organization, visit the website heartsandhooves.com.

Cancer, like many diseases, is a vile foe. How wonderful it would be if we could spend all the money, power, and energy on medical research that we spend blowing human beings apart, waging war, and ruining our planet.

SIMILAR SCENES ABOUND IN AND AROUND SEDONA.

XXIX.
MAGICAL SEDONA

PLACES OF MYSTERIOUS OR POWERFUL ENERGY are not necessarily places in some wilderness. They can be in cities, towns, and even in small villages. They can be in places within these places. I taught at colleges and universities for eighteen years. Each of these institutions had its own energy, and within each of these schools, each particular class had its own energy. Some were uplifting. Some were foreboding. Some were joyful. Some were depressing.

I am an artist. I sculpt and I paint. At one time or another, I have probably been associated with well over fifty galleries. I can assure you, there are different energies in each one. I dreaded walking through

the doors of some of them. There are others that have drawn me into
their confines because they make me feel like "I have gone home." Two
of these are in Arizona. One is the Karin Newby Gallery in Tubac. I
have been affiliated with this gallery since 1988, although I did not visit
it until sometime in the mid 1990s. When I did, I kicked myself for
not having done so sooner. There is a beautiful aura all about the place,
and something within it fills me with energy and with the ambition to
create.

A few hours drive to the north of Tubac is Sedona. Sedona,
Arizona! What a magical place!

> In Sedona Arizona
> Beneath a starry sky
> Red rocks all around me
> I hear the creatures of the night
>
> The wind softly murmurs
> Singing through the trees
> In Sedona Arizona
> Land of ancient peace
>
> Daybreak in the desert
> And I wake up all alone
> The last star has faded
> It's drier than a bone
>
> The desert has its mysteries
> And seldom reveals
> The secrets and the treasures
> That are hidden in its hills
>
> The reckless and the careless
> Die stranded in its wastes
> Lost within confusion
> Of their minds
>
> In endless desperation
> Not knowing they could find
> Eternal sustenance

Within the sands of time

You've got to have faith
You've got to believe
You've got to watch out for illusions
And things that mislead

There's a wide path to nowhere
Paved by those who've failed
The road to where you want to be
Is along some desert trail

Nothing's ever easy
If it's really worth a damn
And few folks know what
Anything's really worth

There's a hundred thousand graveyards
Filled with lonely souls
Escaping and fulfilling
Obligations of their births

Survival in the desert
Is a skill to carefully learn
You can meet the unexpected
At almost every turn

The wasteful soon grow weary
And wither in its sands
Not knowing every need
Is right before their hands

You've got to have faith
You've got to believe
You've got to watch out for illusions
And things that mislead

There's a wide path to nowhere
Paved by those who've failed
The road to where you want to be

Is along some desert trail

In Sedona Arizona
The red rocks speak to me
I hear secrets whispered
As the wind blows through the trees

Ancient people told their stories
They carved them in the stone
With their spirits all around me
This desert is my home

In Sedona, Arizona
The wind blows wild and free
Along these desert trails
Is the place I want to be

Arizona presents a paradox to me, or at least something that seems like one. If it does not present a paradox, it at least presents a mild dilemma. As I write this, I am in Santa Fe, the village of Holy Faith. For centuries something about this area has compelled people to dwell here. It still pulls them in. They leave their homes in the East and move to Santa Fe. They leave their homes in California and move to Santa Fe. They come from the South. They come from the Midwest. They come to Santa Fe from all over the planet because there is magic here and energy here that is appealing to almost everyone who visits this wonderful place. For me it is captivating. It has been since my first visit in the 1950s. I cannot explain this energy, but I can feel it and I bask in it. I watched a spectacular storm roll in a few hours ago. Before my very eyes I saw the energy change. The sky turned the color of blue steel in the west, so dark I became a bit alarmed. The clouds and the wind rolled in, bringing thunder and rain. The rain changed to sleet and covered the ground. The temperature dropped into the low 40s. The piñon logs crackled and popped as they burned in my fireplace, filling the room with their fragrance. The energy was awesome. Then the sun broke through, illuminating the mountains in the east, and the landscape became bright and produced a vivid rainbow. A short time later, there came more clouds, and then the sun again. I am certain such happenings

are a vital part of the energy that has lured people to this place for
centuries.

I am in love with Santa Fe and with my little adobe house
there. I am in love with my studio and my ranch in Texas and with
the surrounding Texas Hill Country. I am in love with Arizona and
the wonderfully picturesque village of Sedona. How do I caress them
all simultaneously? I must take care not to become a peripatetic! But
Sedona! Sedona is magic!

While returning from a show in La Jolla, California, in the late
1980s, I made my initial odyssey to the quaint village named after the
pioneer woman, Sedona Schnebly. There I met with the woman who
became the rep of what some refer to as my "jewelry." She introduced
me to a gallery owner in the village, thereby beginning my odysseys in
and around the quaint and then sleepy village of Sedona.

I could not start to name or list the wonderful people I have
met in the galleries of this charming place. Some have become very dear
personal friends. This, of course, is another part of the mystery, magic,
and energy of Sedona and the surrounding landscape.

In 2003, on a brisk Sunday October morning just following
my eighth annual show at Exposures Gallery, I baptized a friend and
his fiancée in the chilly waters of Oak Creek at Red Rock Crossing,
which is just below Cathedral Rock. We sensed it as a place of energy.
It is proven by the fact that thousands of people visit the site every year.
In fact, the once sleepy village of Sedona now attracts over four million
visitors each year. That should be statement enough that there are
compelling forces in and about the place. For me this is not even subject
to argument. But some things are arguable: things such as vortexes. Do
vortexes really exist? And if they do, then what is a vortex? The vast
amount of hype, the gross amount of print, and the seemingly non-
ending prattle about Sedona vortexes inspired this book.

Are there really "a bunch of vortexes" around Sedona? Some
individuals swear there are. Some say the notion is folly. Some are
skeptical yet at the same time claim to be open-minded. Vortexes are
mysteries; we can be certain of that. If they were not, then there would

not be such argument and speculation about them: about whether they are a reality or a figment of imaginations. If anything, vortexes are undisputedly a mystery around the Red Rock Country of Sedona. On practically any day, people hike on top of the red rock escarpments at places that have been "declared" to be vortexes, or that might be vortexes, or that are vortexes—or that are not vortexes. I do not know who determines the what and where of vortexes. Supposedly, vortexes are swirling, whirling, and spiraling fields of psychic, spiritual energy that interact with a person's inner self. If this is true, then perhaps locating and/or determining a vortex or vortexes is a personal quest. As for me, I have been to "vortex sites" about Sedona, and I have stood in what I was told was their center. I did not feel anything any different from what I generally feel at many places in or around Sedona. I did not feel a trace of negative energy, but I was not gyrated into a state of euphoria, at least nothing apart from my usual, non-drug produced high.

The late J. Frank Dobie, an author famous for his stories and writings of lore about the Southwest, once said, "If the story is not true, it is at least true that it is a story." By the same line of reason, I consider that if the Sedona vortexes are not real, they are nevertheless realities that exist in the minds of believers.

Here again, I remind the reader, *caveat emptor,* and *caveat lector!* This book is in no way an attempt to be scholarly. That was admitted at the onset. Do not look to the scientific community for metaphysical answers. I am grateful to it for many things, yet I would admonish it for sometimes being devoid of spirituality and for often being too dogmatic. I would scold it a bit for generally discarding considerations relating to the spiritual realm. The scientific community oftentimes assumes it is infallible. Some of us admonish it for generally being closed-minded to questions surrounding metaphysical mysteries. The same holds true in my mind for most "organized" religious entities, or at least those that have closed minds to many scientific facts and discoveries. And the same holds true for people in any community who are unwilling to address certain metaphysical mysteries or consider any question contrary to their established beliefs.

Questions surrounding mysteries! I love them! Give me fewer

answers and more questions, more mysteries. What among the vast realm of answers is not an opinion anyway? At least what subjective answers are not opinions? Consider good art and bad art. Which is which? Is the Mona Lisa good art? I personally do not consider it "good art," while at the same time I think it is not "bad art." Good or bad, I would not care to have breakfast beneath it every morning for the following twenty-five years, or even for the next one year. I much prefer something that captures the spirit and energy of the wonderful American Southwest. I would much prefer a work by Helen Frankenthaler or Robert Motherwell or even a landscape by Jan Meyers, Jim Rabby, Doug West, or Paul Milosevich. This is not so much a digression as it might seem to be. Subjectivity is a part of the soul of creative minds. Subjectivity is interwoven with mystery and with creative energy. Questions and beliefs surrounding vortexes are subjective.

Are there vortexes within and around the Red Rocks of Sedona? If so, what are they? Where are they? How does one locate them? Are they constant, or are they in flux like magnetic north? At some points, I feel I am in possession of the transmitter and am lacking the receiver. At other times, I might feel I have the receiver but wonder, where is the transmitter? Here is a paraphrasing of conversations I have had several times:

"Hi! How have you been?"

"Fine, how are you?"

"I'm doing great. What have you been up to?"

"The usual. Work. A little play. I did go on a vacation."

"You did? Where?"

"Oh, I went out to Scottsdale, Tubac, the Grand Canyon, and I went to Sedona, too."

"Sedona? Wow! What a great place! Did you visit any of the vortexes?"

"The what?"

"The vortexes."

"I don't think so. What is a vortex?"

I then explain and elaborate briefly about the theories and notions of the Red Rock vortexes. This is usually followed by a response similar to:

"I *knew* there was something different about that place!"

This person then becomes a convert and also becomes a proselytizing neophyte who espouses the mysteries of the vortexes in and around Sedona.

Well, I knew there was something different about the place, too, and I did not know what it was, or what they were: that thing or those things that for me made Sedona a "different place." It was not vortexes around Sedona that captured me. It was the red rocks. It was Oak Creek. It was Cathedral Crossing. It was the art galleries. It was the clean crisp air, with a faint scent of pine trees.

But what about vortexes? *What is a vortex?* One of my friends wrote a book titled What is a Vortex? Thousands of these books have been sold, but the book does not answer the question it asks. It dances and skirts all around its premise like a baited hook of disclaimers. Ah! I have the answer. Continue reading.

What is a vortex? If you have seen a smoke ring, you have seen a vortex. What makes this visible are the unburned hydrocarbons that are contained within this field of force: that whirling, rotating, invisible ring of gas. You are not seeing a vortex. You are seeing matter born upon or within a vortex.

A simple way to create or generate a wind vortex without smoking (thereby not placing your good health and that of those around you at risk) is to purchase the cheapest one-pound can of coffee you can locate, remove the plastic top, and open the can. Pour the bad coffee out in the flowerbed. This is good for the earth and for the worms. Then, turn the can over and cut or drill a large hole in the center of the metal bottom—say a hole one and a half to two inches in diameter. Replace the plastic lid and then strike this lid with a spoon or a drumstick or something. Instantly, you have generated a ring vortex. It is traveling fast, too. You don't believe me, do you? You can't see it, so you doubt it is there, just like some people might doubt the radio waves they cannot see.

To remove your doubts, have someone stand across the room. Then point the hole in the can toward him and strike the plastic lid forcefully. He will not see it either, but he will feel it. Have this person point or aim the device at you and likewise strike the plastic diaphragm. Then you, too, will feel the vortex. Place a lighted candle on a stand across the room with nothing between it and your new wind vortex-generating device. Strike the plastic cover. You will learn to properly aim this little gadget after a few tries, and you will be amazed that you can quickly blow out a candle from across the room. I mean quickly because the ring vortex travels very swiftly. In fact, watch the toy market for a new toy that operates on this principle. I purchased one at The Fun Store in Sedona. It will blow a hat off someone's head at a surprising distance.

Every time you are in the presence of a live band with a drummer, and the drummer is playing an open base drum, you are being bombarded with vortexes. You cannot see them, you usually do not consciously feel them, but they are there, and they are just as real as their accompanying sounds.

If you have ever seen or witnessed a tornado, you have seen a vortex. If you have ever seen a whirlwind or a so-called dust devil, you have seen a vortex. Again, you have not seen the actual vortexes. They are invisible. As with the unburned hydrocarbons carried in the previously mentioned smoke ring, what you have seen is the moisture, the sand, the dust, or the debris that has been carried by the invisible winds of the vortexes.

Fill your sink with water and then pull the stopper or the plug and you will perceive a vortex, one that will rotate one direction north of the equator and the opposite direction south of the equator. This is known as the "Coriolis Effect," or the "Coriolis Force," whereby rotations are to the right in the northern hemisphere and to the left in the southern hemisphere. Early sailors used the understanding of this as an equatorial locator when they were at sea. The philosophical question here is this: is the vortex visible or is it invisible? Is the vortex the swirling and rotating water, or is it the space within the swirling water? Either way I believe in it.

I believe in spirits, and I believe in vortexes. I believe in radio waves. I believe in jet streams and oceanic currents. I believe in electricity, and I have, since I connected with a short circuit at age four, back in Colorado City, Texas. I remember that event to this day! I believe in light, even when I cannot see it. Look upward on a moonless night. What you will perceive is sunlight viewed from a right angle, or a severely obtuse angle. You are looking at light waves from the side. You cannot see them because they are not reflecting off objects in a manner that strike your retinas enabling you to see them. That is why darkness appears to surround the moon and the planets. There is actually a lot of light around them that the eye cannot perceive. But look at the same illuminating sun's light waves from a 180-degree angle, and they will blind you.

I believe in a lot of things I cannot see. I believe in fear. I believe in Joy. I believe in Love. I believe in LIGHT, even when there is darkness. I believe in vortexes. I believe in God, The Great Spirit. I believe in Existence even though I cannot comprehend how it came to be or how God came to be "I AM." I believe there is no such thing as nothingness and that there has never been such a thing as nothingness, even though I cannot prove this. I simply have not ever been able to see nothing. (And that is not a grammatically incorrect statement!)

I would submit this caveat: do not rely on anyone but yourself to discover a vortex, not any more than you would rely on someone else to tell you when you are in love, or to rely on someone else to tell you what tastes good, or to rely on someone else to tell you what movie or music or book is good or is not good. Don't rely on some atheist to guide you into a realm of spirituality or some Elmer Gantry to lead you into New Testament theology. And don't rely on someone else to tell you what is good art and what is bad art. The only things critics know is what they care for or do not care for, just like it is with you and with me, yet there are people stupid enough to pay them to voice their opinions. A true or genuine critic is someone to aid or assist you in determining _why_ you do or do not care for some artistic work, regardless of what the genre, and regardless of how he or she (the critic) might feel about what you do or do not like.

Here is a suggestion about Sedona, its mysteries, and its vortexes. Go alone or with your soul mate, your lover, your significant other, or a friend to some of the places around the area. Do not talk loudly or excessively. Do not take disc players, iPods, cellular telephones, or other sound generators. Walk softly. Be present in your disposition and be dignified in your posture. Be open-minded to any spiritual insights or occurrences but do not attempt to create things you do not sense or conjure up things that do not exist. Seek as much isolation as is possible from crowds, from groups, or from chattering tourists. _Caveat emptor,_ and _caveat lector_ about anything you purchase, or anything you are given to read, or anything you hear about vortexes and/or energy fields within the Red Rocks of Sedona. There is a paradox here because if you read this and heed the caveats, then you might not follow the suggestions. Hopefully this paradox will not impede your odyssey.

I believe if you seek the Truth, then some day you will know the Truth, and the Truth will endow you with freedom. If you have an open mind, some day you will experience revelation. It might come in a dream. It might appear in a moment of personal insight. It might be revealed as you are driving down some highway. It might even appear to you as you stroll around the Red Rocks or as you stand in awe in some magical place contained within the majesty and the beauty of the ancient escarpments of Sedona, Arizona.

ANTIQUE STOVE
FILE CABINET.

XXX.
THE STEEL TRAP

HERE IS ANOTHER SEDONA STORY. Although I have many
favorite and somewhat insane stories this one has to be among the
richest of them all. It is true, just as all of these other stories are true.
When this particular Sedona episode began, it was dark, dark-thirty at
home at New Art. I was busy sculpting wax when the telephone rang.
I think the caller's name was Virginia, but the truth is I really do not
remember her name for certain. I had absolutely no intention of being
rude to this woman—to that voice on the phone, to whomever it might
belong—but somehow, some way, the conversation deteriorated. This is
not to admit that I was rude, rather a bit iconoclastic; I was firm in my

171

position.

Virginia probably had obtained my name and telephone number from our gallery affiliate in Sedona, the place she said she was calling from.

"I am calling to ask if you would donate a sculpture to our anti-steel animal trap campaign. We are going to have an auction to raise funds in attempts to prohibit the use of steel traps in Arizona."

Instantly, questions began flooding my mind. The primary one concerned how the money was to be used. Were they going to bribe some legislator? Were they going to hire a lobbyist? What kind of auction? Would it be like so many of these, where an artist donates a five thousand dollar item, and it would be sold for less than the foundry costs?

My response was, "I might. I have some sympathy for your cause, but I do not want to become a hypocrite."

"How would you do that?" she queried.

"Because I use steel traps," I replied.

"You do?!" she gasped.

"I must admit that I do," I said, "although it grieves me to do so. In fact, I set one just two nights ago."

There is a certain silence people sometimes manifest that makes me instantly know they are not appreciative of what I am saying or that they are shocked by my statements. I could tell Virginia was not singing in harmony.

"You did?!" she gasped. "What for?"

"Well, I have this old Magic Chef antique stove. It is in mint condition. I use the oven as a place to keep my stationary, stamps, and envelopes. A little deer mouse has taken residence therein, and it urinates upon, defecates upon, and chews holes into some very expensive items, so I set a trap for the little bastard! It is not totally a steel trap, but it is steel and wood. I set it, then I went over to the house, climbed the ladder to the loft, and after a long hard day went to bed. I was dog-tired, but I couldn't get that cute little mouse off my mind. I thought about its little back or neck being smashed and broken when the trap sprang. Blood would begin oozing from its orifices, and it would kick and thrash about for a while in hopeless, agonized attempts to escape the jaws of death. Then its sphincters would relax, and there would be even more mess to clean up.

"I dragged my butt out of the sublime comfort, descended the ladder, walked through the midnight of my yard over to the studio—hoping I would not step on a rattler—and tripped the trap. I walked back across the yard, climbed the ladder, and went to bed. I told myself I would devise another method. I did.

"I thought about purchasing some glue traps by the trade name of 'Last Step' or 'Tom Cat.' They are not steel traps at all, and in fact they have no moving parts. They are pieces of cardboard covered with the stickiest and gooiest substance you can imagine. They are placed in the rodents' paths or 'right of ways.' The unsuspecting little creatures run over the trap and get stuck. Not only is the glue sticky, it is incredibly strong. I accidentally stepped on one of these traps and had to remove my running shoes to get enough leverage to pull it off. It was like the tar baby. For a while I thought I would have to throw the shoes away. These traps may be advertised as humane, but they produce a horrible death. You can hear the mouse screaming and crying as it struggles in vain to free itself from such a horrible predicament. It takes several hours for the creature to expire, and when death does come, it comes from pure exhaustion, oftentimes within a pool of its own urine mixed with its fecal material. I decided not to take this route. A steel trap is much kinder, and that is why I use them—and will probably use them again."

"What did you do?!" Virginia asked.

"I caught the little bitch with my hands. At least I almost did. I guess you could say I did and I didn't. I saw her creeping about and thought I could grab her. I put my welding gloves on so she would not bite me and lunged for her. The gloves were so thick I could not tell whether I had her or not. When I opened my hands to look, she jumped

THE BEST LAID PLANS OF MICE.

out and ran up the wall. I felt pretty stupid. I was also very amazed at how fast a mouse can run up a vertical stucco wall.

"I did not reset the trap. I bought a box of mothballs and placed them in the oven. That got rid of her. At lease it drove her out of the stove and afforded her the opportunity of nesting in my Arches watercolor paper, which was at another place in my studio. This paper is over ten dollars a sheet. After all of this, my stationary then smelled like a combination of mouse shit and mothballs, and it had fantastic, interesting dark stains on it. They sort of looked like Rorschach ink blots.

"She probably ruined fifty dollars worth of stationary and that much more in stamps. Mice love postage stamps! But my loss was trivial compared to a rancher over in Coke County. Have you ever seen a field with 250 dead lambs killed in a single night by one rogue male coyote?"

She admitted that she had not.

"That coyote wiped out that rancher's profits for the year, and if you had seen it, you might not judge him so harshly for using any means he could devise to exterminate the animal—including steel traps."

Virginia still protested.

"Let me ask you this question, Virginia. Do you swat flies, gnats, and mosquitoes?"

"I used to," she admitted, "but now I just walk over to the door and shoo them off when they light on me."

"Well," I asked her, "do you have a fire place?"

She said, "Yes," so I asked her if she considered how many colonies of insects and how many bugs and spiders she had incinerated by her casual and capricious behavior—her "innocent" burning of logs. Like many people, this woman did not have a clue about how reckless her *modus operandi* had been. If it had not been reckless, it had by all means been classically thoughtless.

"I swat flies and burn logs, and I do it with an awareness that

I am taking lives. You can't drive your car without taking life. Look at your windshield. What do you think those spots are? Do you think you have the right to drive? Have you thought about the lizards and ants you crush? Are you one of those rare individuals that have never hit a bird or some other animal while driving? Let me ask you this, Virginia, have you ever had a shot of penicillin?"

She said she had.

"Do you have any comprehension at all how many organisms or how many individual lives you killed when you did this?"

She was silent for a moment and admitted she had "never thought about it that way." I told her if she would send me some literature on the anti-steel trap campaign, I would read it and consider making a donation. That was years ago. I have not heard from her since.

Virginia, if that is her name, is typical. She is typical of the countless people who crusade for a cause and are blind to the repercussions of their own life styles. She is not a bad person, and neither are the others in her camp. All are just somewhat myopic.

Animal rights people have some wonderful points for all of us to consider. Animals should not be tortured for scientific studies, but humans—who are omnivores, and those of us who use animal products and by-products—are not necessarily torturers. Someone who claims to be vegetarian and who nevertheless eats eggs—eggs not laid by free ranging hens—certainly participates in "torture." Visit a caged layer farm and watch the artificial sunrises and sunsets created by electric lights so that laying hens produce two eggs every day, even when their tired bodies attempt to rest. These birds live in complete captivity. They spend their lives in a small steel cage, never see the natural light of day, and their feet never touch the ground. When they grow old and can no longer lay, they are killed and ground up for food to feed the animal rights peoples' pets, or else they are used for fertilizer to grow produce to feed the vegetarians.

Now I realize that some people are vegetarians due to health reasons or because of a general distaste for meat. However, there are those who are vegetarians because they oppose consuming food produced from living things, but in truth, they are consuming living cells. They abort bean and alfalfa sprouts; they often eat cheeses and consume milk products and think they are vegetarians. They gulp down yogurt and think themselves to be purists. Every time I purchase a box of alfalfa and radish sprouts, I cringe a little as I crunch and munch them with my molars, savoring their delicious juices mixing with my saliva. I usually also ingest some dead turkey. The dead turkey causes me less grief than the living sprouts, sprouts that could have turned a drab brown field into a sea of deep rich green plants with wonderful aromas and vibrant purple flowers. I think of the rows and rows of radishes that could have enjoyed long, wonderful rich growing lives: radishes that could have flowered and brought forth seeds that would produce future plants of their own kind. And there I sit, killing them with my mouth and enjoying the very process that brings them death. And I am so culturally refined that I do not even replenish the earth with my manure. I flush it into a concrete tank instead.

People's lack of consciousness is amazing. Do you want to elevate it? Then go do some research. Learn where red ink comes from. Learn where artists' black paint comes from. Learn where the adhesive on duct tape comes from. Learn about the created life and death you participate in when you drink a glass of wine, a bottle of beer, or a margarita. Learn where silk comes from and how the silkworms are boiled to death. Learn about the animal and plant life killed to obtain the products to manufacture your synthetic world.

If a person were going to be a champion for absolute "fairness" to all life, then his/her life style would be one of total nudity, absolute non-bathing, total fasting, and complete non-mobility. Great Spirit did not so design the world so that life is, or even should be, in this manner. Lions kill and eat zebras. Bears kill and eat salmon. Watch the bears on the Nature Channel. They usually kill them in the process of eating them, stripping the skins from their flipping quivering bodies. Should we go murder the bears for killing and torturing the salmon, and should we murder the lions for killing and eating the zebras? Birds kill and eat insects. Fish kill and eat fish. Some whales kill and eat seals. What should we do about that? Man lives in similar fashion and to refute this (or to even feel guilty about it) is in some manner a way of telling God that He did not do a proper job with creation.

The good news is that there is evolution, and within its processes *homo sapiens* may evolve so that he can eat the dust of this earth and from it derive all the proteins, minerals, and amino acids he requires. The bad news is that it is going to be very difficult to obtain earth dust that does not contain organisms.

A lot of energy has been directed to animal rights controversy, still brewing. It is a mystery of life.

Virginia, or whatever her name is, inspired this story and so did the woman in Tarrytown (in Austin, Texas) who evicted tenants from her shopping center because they use or sell animal products. How greatly I do admire their spirit and intentions. How vast is the gulf of our non-understandings. How great is her courage to stand up for her convictions, but sometimes energies can appear to be misguided.

I wonder if my own energies are misguided. I ponder the issue over and over. I should not judge. However, I am admonished that "by their fruits I shall know them." The question of evaluation versus judgment then comes forth. There is rarely one judgment ever rendered that does not come back to the one who makes the judgment. Yes, even those I am making in this writing! Ah! Let me just label them evaluations because I am not pronouncing or issuing sentences.

XXXI.
THE WINDS
OF FATE

THERE ARE PEOPLE who just do not believe in vortexes, and no one can convince them that they are real. No one has to convince me about the existence of vortexes because once upon a time I was in the edge of a vortex. Then I was in the absolute center of that vortex. Then I was again in the edge of that vortex. Such awesome power the vortexes have, and the one I was in was equivalent in energy to several thousands of tons of dynamite, that marvelous explosive substance invented by the founder of the Nobel Peace Prize! One could well wonder how something could have so much power, especially something as transparent as the wind, and how such an ethereal substance could have such force and carry such destruction, but it can, and it does. Thus another reason I believe in vortexes is because I have been in their epicenters. I have been in several vortex epicenters. Let me tell you about one in particular.

Ted Bell was from Floydada, where he was the United States Postmaster. Floydada, Texas, is about as bald a spot in the bald cotton patch country as one could ever hope to find. It is about forty miles to the east and a bit north of Lubbock. In my consideration Lubbock is not exactly the Garden of Eden, and whatever garden it might be just keeps getting worse the closer to Floydada one gets.

Ted was a somewhat decent watercolor painter, or at least he was on May 11th, 1970, when all of what I am about to relate happened. He came to my house that day for a cold beer and to trade a few painting licks. Then we hopped into his brand new Ford sedan, the one he had purchased that very day, and drove downtown to a meeting of the West Texas Watercolor Society. The event was staged in the ground floor Flame Room of the Pioneer Natural Gas Company, adjacent to the Lubbock National Bank and catty-cornered to the First Methodist Church.

The program was well attended because Robert Woods was demonstrating. This Woods was not to be confused with the Robert Woods who was Porfirio Salinas' teacher, the one who was the painter of seascapes and, most notably, the famed painter of Texas Hill Country bluebonnets. This Robert Woods was from California and was the president of the National Watercolor Society. He was quite skilled as I recall, sloshing juicy washes on full vertical sheets of 300-pound Arches paper with incredible adroitness and amazing control. The washes would have dripped to the floor for anyone else, but for Mr. Woods they tenaciously defied a high percent of gravity, running just enough for excitement then stopping and tricking the eye into believing they were rocks and flowers and trees and various other recognizable objects. Most watercolor painters paint on an almost flat or horizontal surface; thus, we were all amazed to see someone painting on an easel as would an oil painter paint on canvas.

Many residents of Lubbock who could paint—or who thought they could paint, or who wished they could paint—were there, including a good number who knew good and well they could not paint but loved to try anyway. We were all spellbound.

It had been one of those beautiful and splendid spring days on the high plains, and back at my house Ted and I had marveled at the prodigious buildup of cumulus nimbus clouds. The stark, billowing whites and the contrasting grays and ochres against a sparkling blue sky would stir any slumbering spirit and hone to a fine edge the desires of landscape painters such as we were—or such as we wished we were. So Ted and I were already in high spirits, and Robert Woods was making them soar even higher.

When we pulled into a parking space beside the bank building, Ted killed the engine, and I started to get out of his new sedan. He suddenly restarted the engine. I closed the door and asked him what he was doing. "I just did not like that spot," he said, as he drove across Broadway, made a u-turn, and parked beside the First Methodist Church.

The Flame Room adjoined the Lubbock National Bank by a long hallway that was open on both the north and south ends. The site was at Avenue J and Broadway Street. There was a very small kitchen in the southwest corner of the gas company's facility. This area had a cased opening portal adjoining the larger main room. The smaller space was where gas range cooking demonstrations were conducted. The street side of the main room faced north on Main Street and was mostly glass fenestration. Double glass doors opened into another hallway bordered on the east by Avenue J.

Robert Woods painted and the sky darkened. No one seemed to notice that it did. Then it began to get a bit blustery. Sand began blowing down Main Street. A few of us noticed this, but blowing sand in Lubbock is not an uncommon thing, and Robert Woods had us mesmerized. Then a particularly noisy gust of wind blew open the north doors of the east hallway. Sand and dust and trash blasted southward through this area. Clarence Kincaid, Texas Tech art professor, hastily got up and went through the doors that connected the main room (where we were watching the demonstration) to the east hallway in attempts to close the outside doors. Upon reaching them, he immediately turned around and raced back in the opposite direction. He was sprinting. He did not stop and did not pause. He said nothing as he disappeared through another set of doors connecting the space to a south room adjoining the main room. In this quarter a stairway descended into a basement. Kincaid was a most unlikely sprinter because he had experienced a recent heart attack, and he was not supposed to exert himself or get overly excited. His sudden movements flushed everyone from their seats. The spectators at the Wood's demonstration reminded me of a covey of quail: frightened, flushed, and running toward the basement door. Woods joined them in the rear. They were almost trampling one another. I cupped my hands around my mouth and bellowed, "Don't panic!" I was afraid someone was going to be trampled and injured. The only mind they paid me was a few hard glances through very wide eyes, and they continued to push and squeeze and shove themselves though the door.

It was a pathetic scene because many elderly women were intermingled and competing with young college art students. All were animals in flight and in fright, as if there were no age, no social status, or no gender. There was only a herd of panicked, reflexive animals—a seething mass that was composed of fifty or sixty terrified individuals, each possessing one dominant thought: "Me! Survive!"

"Let them go, Ted. Let's go over there. I've always heard that the southwest corner is the safest place." So Ted and I went over to the southwest corner of the small semi-enclosed kitchenette. It was prematurely dark outside, and there was a greenish-black glow over Main Street and the buildings beyond. There was noise! It was a loud howling noise. It was not just the noise of panicked people overturning chairs, praying and crying and singing hymns in fear, but the sound of creaking doors, of falling hail, and wailing, moaning, groaning, howling winds.

Ted and I sat down on the floor in the kitchenette by the metal cabinets. The sounds escalated. The sounds soared and roared. The noise was louder than a freight train. It roared as ten freight trains would roar.

"Are you scared?" I asked Ted.

"Yea, kinda," he replied. "Are you?"

"Hell yes, I'm scared!" I replied.

He lit a cigarette and gave me one. I didn't have much heart for it, but I took it and lit it. The storm was awesome. The plate glass windows were effortlessly sucked from their sockets, making a not too audible "plink" sound. The curtains rose to 180 degrees within the room. They were sticking straight out from their supporting rods. Then we watched in amazement as they frayed apart and unraveled, thread by thread. Brochures, programs, and full sheets of Arches 300 pound watercolor paper, along with Robert Woods' exhibit of paintings, arose from the tables and levitated in a slow counter-clockwise rotation around the room.

It was as if there was no gravity, for all manner of things were floating in the air as if some magician had suspended them there. Ted and I watched these strange events through the cased openings of the Flame Room kitchen.

There were metal cabinets in the room. At one point I tried to crawl into them after removing some drawers, but it was too tight a fit. I could not squeeze into the space. I imagined rescue people attempting to remove my body from such a mangled, twisted conglomeration of wrecked steel structures. I took comfort that, the day before, I had purchased a $50,000 life insurance policy. That was about the only secure feeling that I had, knowing my children would be provided for.

After what was probably less than ten minutes, but what seemed more like two or three hours, the roar ceased and the papers and the other objects settled gently to the floor. We survived! Ted and I survived! We got to our feet, a bit shakily. Hearing voices and hard heels on concrete, I cautiously attempted to open the steel door of the kitchenette. It adjoined the open-air west mall way. It would not budge. The doorframe had been twisted out of shape. I kicked it open.

There was a dead calm. There was not even a breeze. A few people were talking as they were briskly walking or wading southward through the hallway next to the bank, wading in twelve-inch deep water. As Ted and I were getting our adrenalin stabilized, we began to hear it again—that dreadful roar. It was growing louder and louder. Pieces of paper and debris began blowing from the main room through our little kitchen sanctuary and out the portal we had opened. With difficulty, I pulled at the small, very slick metal doorknob to secure the door. The incredible pressure and force of the storm had sprung either the door or its casing, and it just simply would not close! The force of blowing, sucking wind would not allow me to hold it for long, either.

"Ted, see if there is a towel in that drawer! Hurry!" Ted quickly fumbled around, found one, and handed it to me. I looped it over and around the outside knob and pulled at the door. Something hit it on the outside that sounded like a rifle shot. It was some item being blown through the hallway by the hundred-mile-an-hour winds. A few seconds earlier it would have either killed me or broken my bones while I was looping the towel around the doorknob.

I wrist-locked the towel, sat on the floor, and placed my boots against the frame. I was very strong at the time, yet it was all I could do to hold on. Ted reached around my back and grabbed hold. Together we did it! We held on, and for days afterward our forearms were sore from the strain.

The panicked crowd had found its way to the basement, a much safer and drastically less dramatic position than was ours. There, we were told, they held hands, prayed, and sang hymns.

Ted and I gathered the paintings of Robert Woods. He was dashing about from place to place with his sketchbook, manically sketching this wreckage and that wreckage. He was calm, and he was frantic. I was in awe, and Ted Bell was ready to go back to Floydada. Power lines were down. There was deep water in the streets. There were sirens, flashing red and blue lights, and muttering voices. It was by far the most chaos I had ever witnessed.

The clad marble sheets that adorned the Lubbock National

Bank and the Pioneer Natural Gas company buildings had collapsed. Most of that marble sheeting had fallen off the sides of the buildings and had flattened the vehicle now parked in the space where Ted had first parked. I do not remember what kind of vehicle it was, but it was reduced to about two feet high with a stack of stone debris on its top. Ted's brand new Ford sustained only minor scratches and a cracked windshield. By the time we reached his car, stations around the country were already broadcasting the event of the storm. The telephone lines were down, so it was impossible to call my parents in Colorado City, one hundred miles to the south. Ted was somehow able to call his family in Floydada and let them know he was safe. I think that was the last time I saw Ted. That was May 11, 1970. I later learned that Ted died in 1977, the same year my father died. He was a fine gentleman, and he truly had the spirit of an artist.

Another of my friends, Jim Eppler, was at the watercolor demonstration. He was only nineteen years of age. I had met him when giving him his first watercolor lessons. He was too shaken up to drive, so I drove his car and took him to his house. I called another friend who picked me up there and took me to my house, four miles to the west. The only damage there was a fence blown down. That was not the case in downtown Lubbock. A monumental sculpture, created by Forrest Gist and Lonny Edwards for the Fields Company, was wrecked beyond restoration. An unbroken and unopened bottle of Lone Star Beer had come to rest on top of an open door at a house nearby. The house was wrecked, but the beer was safe. The nearby twenty-storied Great Plains Life Building was twisted. The Lubbock National Bank Building, adjacent to the watercolor society meeting, was almost in ruins. The bank president's desk was gone. It had been sucked out of the building and blown away—so it was reported—as was a two-ton press at the nearby Hancock Manufacturing Company. A dozen eggs were the only undestroyed things in another Lubbock dwelling.

Twenty-one people were killed as a result of the storm; one hundred were injured. The damage was estimated at multiple millions of dollars. All this was remarkably low considering the intensity of the storm and the dense population where it struck. It was the "Lubbock Tornado," as it is named, and it is estimated the twister was one half mile in diameter. The speculation is that the first roar was the leading edge of the tornado, that awesome vortex. As it passed to the northeast, the center of the vortex was the "dead calm" that we experienced, and the second roar was the backside of the funnel. These days, that storm is a celebrated event. The annual "Lubbock Tornado Jam" memorializes it.

Time marches on, and it became May 11, 1999, twenty-nine years to the day after the Lubbock tornado. My telephone rang at New Art. It was my friend and colleague, sculptor Gene Tobey.

"Hey Worrell, this is Gene Tobey. I just saw on the news that there is a tornado on the ground at Castell!" Castell is on Ranch Road 152 and down-river about seven miles from my house and studio. It was a hot spring day. I was wearing cut-offs. I grabbed some jeans and a shirt and blasted out of my driveway and then up the hill a mile away where my then assistant, Michelle Blair, and her two daughters lived. They were in a state of terror. I took them to the Dairy Queen in Mason, bought them a treat, then headed on out to Tobey's house and studio four miles north of town. There, it was still and calm. It was so quiet and peaceful we could have no comprehension of the violence then occurring on the Llano River. That twister hit on the same date, May 11, and at almost the same exact hour that the Lubbock Tornado had struck twenty-nine years before.

I drove back home about sundown and was going to check on the Evans, my neighbors a mile to the east. The road was blocked by an uprooted live oak tree, one some four feet in diameter. I was going to walk on to their house, but Willow Creek was flooding, and to get across I would have to wade or swim and fight no telling how many water moccasins. I returned to my house and thanked God that New Art had been spared. The carcass of that huge tree is still there beside Lower Willow Creek Road, one mile east of my studio and residence.

The following morning I picked up my neighbor, Wallace Bosse. We drove across the Llano River Bridge on Highway 87 and turned east on Ranch Road 152. What we saw was shocking. The vista more resembled a lunar landscape than the usual bucolic Texas Hill Country. There was a half-mile long strip where the pavement had been ripped away by the wind. Houses and barns were gone. What were once prodigious centuries-old live oak trees were now leafless stumps. The ground was bare, stripped of every blade of grass and all vegetation. Dead livestock littered the ranchland. Flies were already buzzing around cow carcasses that had not a hair left on their bodies. Some had been pierced through both sides by large tree branches. Gophers, snakes, and other small animal bodies were scattered around. The only thing remaining of the Mayfield Kothmann ranch house was the concrete windmill tower. His prized Indian artifact collection was scattered by the winds of the storm. Days later someone found one of his old cancelled checks, dated in the 1940s, in a cemetery at Rockport, Texas, on the Gulf Coast some 250 miles to the south.

Had this twister hit ten or twelve miles to the northwest, it would have destroyed the town of Mason. As it was, it left a half-mile wide swath of denuded landscape almost to Loyal Valley, some six miles south of where it first touched ground. Amazingly, there was only one human injury. This injury later became a fatality due to infection. A plank of torn timber impaled an eighty-year-old rancher. He died a few weeks later in a San Angelo hospital.

The scars from that storm still remain along Ranch Road 152. These days residents along Lower Willow Creek Road pay a great deal of attention when *cumulonimbus* clouds begin building up in the springtime Hill Country sky. We all are forever watchful for the Winds of Fate.

Now you ask me, "Do you believe in vortexes?" My answer is, "I do, brother, I do!"

THESE PHOTOS SHOW THE RIVER HAS CHANGED. IT USED TO BE ABOUT 100 YARDS WIDE AT THESE SPOTS. I CAUGHT LOTS OF FISH THERE WHEN I WAS A KID. IT TEAMED WITH RED HORSE MINNOWS...WE HAVE NOT SEEN ONE OF THOSE FISH IN YEARS.

XXXII.
MITCHELL COUNTY,
TEXAS

WE WERE ALWAYS OUT FOR ADVENTURE, or thought we were, or thought that if we made a strong enough pretense about it, someone might think we were—and would thereby be impressed. Most likely, we just thought we were. We really scarcely knew what adventure was because our world was quite limited and so very small. Adventure for us was catching rats with fishing tackle in the Ritz Theatre—until Elliott Dixon, the owner, made us quit because he said it was bad for business. They were big rats, too! They would run across people's feet as they sat and watched Gene Autry, Roy Rogers, The Durango Kid, Wild Bill Elliott, Hopalong Cassidy, and other B-rated movies.

There were holes in the lobby floor, and in the hidden chambers beneath them lurked the huge rats, grown fat by feeding upon spilled popcorn and other things moviegoers left on the floor. It was through these holes that we caught the rats. We baited the hooks with crickets, cheese, or popcorn. It was a bit like ice fishing, or at least we thought it to be.

To us adventure was hiking and fishing on Lone Wolf Creek or on the Colorado River that flows through Mitchell County. Our adventures were certainly not so daring as Craig Child's in his book, *The Secret Knowledge of Water,* as he was creeping into a spring-fed waterfall high on the cliffs of the Grand Canyon above a different Colorado River. Ours were nothing comparable to the either brave or capricious wanderings and forays of Edward Abbey. We thought leaping across the sandstone narrows and chasms at Seven Wells on Champion Creek was daring. Perhaps it was, when one considers that had we come short on our jumps from precipitous sandstone ledge to precipitous sandstone ledge, a fall of fifty feet would likely be no less fatal than one of a hundred feet. We were also gutsy enough to pick up rattlesnakes and put them in gunnysacks. Some of those diamondbacks were six feet long. Once, while we were fooling around with our bows and arrows out on the Cuthbert flats, we caught one a bit over six feet in length. Its head was as large as my hand with fingers doubled at the second joint. We had no gunnysack with us at the time, so we broke a piece of wire from a fence and lashed the reptile to a mesquite stick. Then we placed it in the car trunk. When we showed it off in town that evening to some of the men gathered at the Best Yet Café, they thought we were crazy. We were.

We did our fair share of exploring the old salt mine near Colorado City, going through scores of abandoned homesteads, and prowling in a goodly number of what were reported to be haunted houses and buildings. Sometimes we would visit these in the dark of night—without flashlights. Each of those places had an intriguing aura and energy. Each had its own mystery, power, or energy, or all three of these.

But the Colorado River had its own special energy; it has for millenniums. From its beginning spring in Northwest Texas to where it dumps into the Gulf of Mexico in Southeast Texas, it has its own energy. Its banks are strewn almost continuously with the litter and debris of ancient Indian campsites, some over eight thousand years old.

In our adolescent days, we would roam its banks and pick up sacks full of these flint artifacts. This was from surface finds and not from grave lootings or excavations. Artifact collecting has always been a matter of intrigue, curiosity, and bewilderment to me. When John Q. Citizen hunts arrowheads, if he excavates or if he loots ancient graves, then he is a vandal. That is, he is a vandal in the opinions of university archaeology professors and museum curators. If a university archaeology professor or someone from a museum does the same thing, then he is a scientist. The latter most often hoards and stores his booty in dark basement vaults, far from the visibility of the public.

Sometimes the energy of this river, this used-to-be-wonderful river, visits me in my dreams and in my slumbers. I again see the astronomical quantities of flint chips and artifacts that rested on its ridges and on its second banks. There was magic in picking up a flint point, a blade, or any ancient artifact for that matter and later learning that likely I was the first human to handle it or touch it for the past two to six thousand years.

The Colorado River was wide and shallow with occasional deep holes. There were legends about people drowning in these holes, and there were stories of people sinking to their deaths beneath quicksand. Ghostly tales, they were. It was a flowing river. It housed an incredible multitude of aquatic species, including the spectacular red horse minnow. It was rich with catfish of several varieties. It held black bass, drum, needle-nosed gar, various bream and bluegills, freshwater clams, and crayfish.

In the 1920s or '30s, the Anderson-Pritchard Petroleum Company established the Col-Tex Refinery on the western banks of this stream. The business was within the township of Colorado, Texas, now known as Colorado City. From 1924 until 1969, this refinery severely polluted the Colorado River. There were forty-five years of oil, tar, and gasoline that seeped into the ground. There was also deliberate dumping of waste onto the riverbank and even dumping into the river itself. There was no EPA in those days. The townspeople tolerated the abuse because it was the main economy of the community. I do not know why the state tolerated it. To this day, that now defunct and non-existent refining establishment pollutes the river, even though it closed operations nearly a half-century ago.

Additionally, the dam vandals constructed impoundments along the river's course, several of them. Almost at its emergence in Dawson County, there is a dam. There is another dam about three miles northwest of Colorado City. At Robert Lee, an enormous dam created what is called Lake Spence. This inundated countless ancient Indian campsites and laid down enormous silt beds on what is once again attempting to be a desert floor. Lake Ivy follows Spence, and then there is Lake L.B.J., which formerly had the enchanting and descriptive name of Granite Shoals. Lake Buchanan is next, then Lake Inks, Lake Travis, Lady Bird Johnson Lake, and Lake Buescher. Of course, these are not lakes at all. They are reservoirs or impoundments, and they have certainly changed the energy of the Colorado River and its tributaries. And now political agencies have been created—bureaucracies, they are—which regulate, govern, control, and have power and dominion over almost everything and anything that touches the Colorado River in any way.

There were places in Mitchell and Coke Counties where the flowing water was 100 yards wide, filled with vast schools of teaming minnows and various fishes. It is now a narrow, choked, silt-laden bed, barely trickling, and infested with tamarisk or salt cedar trees imported from the Mediterranean. They were brought in by the government to "control erosion" and have invaded almost every stream in the American West and Southwest. This river's energy, magic, and power has been changed and altered drastically by human beings.

In the 1950s the pollution was really bad. It came from the refinery and from countless upstream oil wells, but the river was nevertheless still wide and it was still flowing. When it rained—I mean when a real gully washer came—the volume of water flooding through its channels was awesome to behold. Half the town would gather at the Highway 80 Bridge on the west side of Colorado City just to view the turbulent and muddy waters of the flood.

It was on one such occurrence that Danny Majors and I decided to float it. We borrowed an eight-foot plywood dingy from Billy Bobo, and in this we made our odyssey. We started about four o'clock on a midsummer's afternoon a scant few miles south of town, on Charley Thompson's ranch. We took a couple of Cokes each, some cans of Vienna sausage, some crackers, and a package of Oreo Cookies.

We thought we had a good idea about how far it was from where we put in on the Thompson Ranch to where we were going to take out on the Spade Ranch—but we didn't. We just presumed it would be a similar distance as was the drive by road. We roughly (and incorrectly) calculated this to be fewer than twenty miles. We guessed the river's waters to be clipping along about ten to twelve miles an hour, so we doubled the time we thought it would take and calculated we would reach Pecan Crossing before or around 8:00 p.m., when it would still be daylight. This was wrong!

Alas! The water moved faster than our craft. This raging torrent simply outran us. I was a strong man with unbelievable endurance. So was Danny, but even with a good set of oars and locks, the water passed us by. It must have been similar to having a surfboard on the backside of a breaker.

The Cokes vanished. The Vienna sausage and crackers vanished. The Oreos vanished. The sun vanished—vanished slowly—but it vanished nevertheless. Darkness fell, and it fell hard. It was dark upon dark. The river was black, or nearly black. Every now and then we would catch a reflected glint from the last of twilight, but not often because we were in the channel of the river and that is always the lowest point of the surrounding landscape. Above us a million suns blazed brightly. We knew there were enormous suns out there in the vast distance, but by the time their light reached us—after eons of travel through space—they did not give all that much illumination. At their astronomical distances, they did not cast enough brilliance for us to see anything. We continued on our odyssey, mostly by faith and by trusting that the current would probably carry the boat over the most favorable water.

We rowed and rowed, spelling each other. We rowed for two or three centuries, maybe more, in a world that had no familiarity. It had no familiarity because we were customarily prowling along the banks and not in the streambed.

The state of our ship was slowing. The river was black. The sky was only a shade or two lighter than black. Within the ship were two weary children—hungry, thirsty children, with unknown miles to go. But we had faith! We had the faith that children have knowing and believing that someday school would be out. Summer would come and with it would come the vacationing freedom we had known. Before too long—we did not know how long—recess would arrive.

The bell rang our vacation—our recess—at Beal's Creek. Beal's Creek is a tributary that originates somewhere near Big Spring, Texas, some fifty or sixty miles northwest of where we were. It was on such a rampage that we could hear it long before we arrived at its turbulent mouth. It merges with the Colorado River at an almost right angle from the southwest, about a mile above Pecan Crossing. This was to be our final destination, or at least our takeout point.

At one time in the past, there was, no doubt, a grove of pecan trees at this crossing, but nothing remains of them now. There will probably be another grove there sometime in the future, and then the relentless waters will take it away again. This will be a long, long time away because the dams have to go first so that the cleansing waters can scour the riverbed.

The gunnels on our craft were not a foot tall, and we were afraid we would have to go uphill to get into the roaring rapids that were spilling in from Beal's Creek. This was by all means a place of energy and a place of power. We kept low in the craft and pulled the oars against the current. We got up that "hill" of water and began making really good time! We soon concluded we had passed Pecan Crossing, unable to recognize it in the roaring darkness. We maneuvered over to the north bank and began inching our way back upstream, dragging the craft with a rope. I grabbed the bow painter and bailed out, dragging the craft for another hundred years until we came to the road at the low water crossing. We dragged the boat a couple of hundred yards up the ruts and began hoofing it to the closest ranch house, the place where Bubba Swan lived. This was five or six miles distant.

Bubba worked for the Spade Ranch. He lived in this house and was married to Danny's sister. From there we telephoned for a middle-of-the-night ride back home and drank a cold beer with Bubba. It may have been the best beer I have ever tasted. I think Danny agreed.

Some day, in some other moment of folly, I may make this voyage again—may make it in memory of Danny Majors, my old friend, now deceased.

When I wrote the first draft of this account on 03/09/06, 10:08 p.m., I had just received an e-mail from Marcom Majors, Danny's son, telling me that Danny died that evening at 5:15 p.m. I am crying. That is an energy, too. It is a power. It is a mystery how we can laugh and keep talking, but when we cry everything shuts down. I couldn't talk now if I had to. I have never known a person as tough as Danny Majors, and I have never known a finer human being. Here's to you, Danny, and to your wonderful energy, your power, the mysteries you frequently presented, and your very generous spirit.

XXXIII.
GOD AND THE FALLEN ANGEL

I WAS ABOUT AGE TWELVE when this story happened. I wrote it in my journal some fifteen years ago and wanted to include it in my first book, *Voices From the Caves – The Shamans Speak*. My sister/manager/editor forbade it because she thought it might be offensive to some. I do not think it will because I know that many know that boys will be boys. Boys will be inventive, too, and they were especially inventive in times of World War II, when almost everything was rationed, in short supply, in high demand, and essentially unavailable.

When I was a kid, I could not comprehend human fatigue. I could not imagine why the "old folks" wanted to sit around in chairs on lawns and porches and gab when they could have been out prowling the neighborhood. There was so much to do and to explore! Some of the men would sit around puffing on cigars, and the women would talk about the good old days. At times after dark, we would be fascinated by the glowing embers on the end of their smokes. We would often eavesdrop on them, hoping to hear them cuss or tell dirty stories, and then we would go on about our odysseys.

The neighborhood was a kingdom, especially so in a small town like ours. The days were golden, but of course, back then we just could not see this. There was a haunted house nearby. It was dark and creepy, and there was gold buried somewhere in back of it. We knew for sure there was gold buried there because the big boys told us so. There was not only one haunted house, there were at least two more, and if we would go inside them, be still, and watch and listen, we would see ghosts and hear them moaning and crying. At least that is what the big boys told us.

There was Lone Wolf Creek and the Colorado River to prowl, stores downtown to browse, bows and arrows to make, caves to dig, and all sorts of things to do. Why in the world would anyone want to just sit around and talk and do nothing? There was energy all over the place! We lusted over the goods in the stores. We had little or no money, so we just looked and dreamed. We dug big pits in the vacant lots, threw branches upon them, covered them with newspapers, and then threw the excavated dirt upon the paper. This transformed the excavated pits into fascinating subterranean chambers. They became wonderful haunts, and we would carve niches in the walls and place lighted candles in them. We were absolutely kings!

> We used to wish our childhood days away
> Dreaming dreams of being in some far-away place
> Pretending we were chasing outlaws or sailing pirate seas
> Losing our minds in reveries and make-believes
> While the world went on around us
> And we did not see —

That we were kings

Kings, kings
Kings you and I
Ruling an empire
No gold could ever buy

Kings, kings
Kings you and I
Once we were kings
And we did not realize

We must have had a cloud around our childhood brains
That dulled us to the wonders of our domains
Back alleys of the neighborhood vacant lots and caves
Summer fields and lightning bugs and splashing in the waves
We were free in our childhood days
And we could not see —
Now we're slaves

Saturdays we prowled every store downtown
Spent the afternoons with Hoppy, Gene, and Johnny Mack Brown
And a nickel bag of candy lasted all the movie through
Through Jungle Queen, Don Winslow, Zorro, and Lash LaRue
We were free as free could be
And we did not see —
That we were kings

We had our first chews and cigarettes behind a neighbor's shed
With talk of love and girls and fantasies running through our heads
The smell of summer rain on the hot, thirsty ground
Bullfrogs, fish, and arrowheads, and treasures to be found
And the city swimming pool
Three whole months with no school
Ahhhhh! We were kings

Kings, kings
Kings you and I
Ruling an empire

No gold could ever buy

Kings, kings
Kings you and I
Once we were kings
And we did not realize

There was a hermit by the river in a tarpaper shack
He buried gold at the haunted house with a graveyard in back
We searched and searched and dug and dug not knowing
at the time
The treasure was the looking not the gold we hoped to find
We were free as free could be
And we did not see —
That we were kings

Kings, kings
Kings you and I
Ruling an empire
No gold could ever buy

Kings, kings
Kings you and I
Once we were kings
And we did not realize

We had no way to know back in those childhood days
That time could pass so fast and forever fly away
Now we're scattered like leaves blowing in the winter winds
Like leaves torn from the trees long separated friends
We were free as free could be
Now we can plainly see —
That we were kings

There were also various cubbies and drawers and closets and cabinets
and places to meddle, and meddling was one of my most favorite of all
activities. It was meddling that led me to a remarkable discovery, and
the consequence was to learn that my father was a lot like God. He was
much like the true God of Love and Mercy. My father was also a lot like

the ancient Hebrew God, a God whose wrath was as limitless as was His power.

I was much like the fallen angel. I was born with a quotient for being a perfect model child, and I was also born with a limitless capacity for meddling, mischief, and what was termed naughtiness. In addition, I was born the middle child and had an older genius brother and a younger beautiful sister—the girl my parents had long desired.

It is difficult for me to remember a time during my childhood when I was not in trouble, or about to be in trouble. This forced me into an almost perpetual state of hypocrisy. My father was the city attorney and had a high profile. My siblings were of angelic quality. Because they were so sweet and pure, the local gentry viewed me in a similar light. They could not have been more mistaken, of course, and I certainly knew better. So did God, and so did my father who, much like God, was almost always working. He had very little time for anything other than our mother, his law practice, and the golf course, which he probably considered his extended office. With his high profile and workaholic personality, he certainly had no time, patience, or most of all, tolerance for dealing with embarrassment by a wild young son.

His addiction to his work meant my role models were my brother and the neighborhood kids. This was a Yin and Yang element and produced a perpetual state of schizophrenia because, on one hand, there was my angelic brother, and on the other hand, there were David Kinard and Andy Prather. God could either do absolutely nothing with either one of them, or He simply did not want to be around them. Now, sixty years later, I think it was both!

It was not that I was really evil. I was just very curious and very interested in certain things; these qualities compelled me to explore. This led me to discover all sorts of things, like flaking flint by throwing large nodules of it against the concrete porch in order to produce smaller, more workable pieces. Unfortunately, this caused the concrete porch to also break into small unworkable pieces that were not good for anything and did absolutely nothing to enhance the appearance of the porch.

My explorations and experiments led me to discover I could

melt metal in the coals of a campfire. I could also melt it in tin cans over the fire and pour it into molds I had fashioned. Progressing in my discoveries, I learned I could melt it on Mother's kitchen stove—while she was away, of course. My explorations also led me to invent a very powerful weapon that would hurl projectiles two hundred yards, shoot through one side of a tin can, and through the thickest of glass panes. My insatiable curiosity further led me to discover a box of condoms in my parents' dresser drawer. I did not have a clue as to what they were, but they were absolutely fascinating! They were the most plastic, inflatable, resilient things I had ever encountered, and their capacity for holding water was astounding.

There was a great energy about the country, this United States of America. We sang songs of patriotism: "Over There," by George M. Cohan, "God Bless America," by Irving Berlin, "Coming in on a Wing and a Prayer," by Harold Adamson and Jimmie McHugh. We sang other songs of freedom such as "My country, 'tis of thee, Sweet land of liberty, Of thee I sing." We sang these in school, and we heard them on the AM radio as they blended in with the almost always-present static. FM radio was way in the future.

It was energy of bonding and of patriotism. It was a united effort to defeat Adolf Hitler, Benito Mussolini, and Hirohito and to save the free world. We were allied with France, Britain, Australia, and other countries. American citizens were mashing tin cans flat and taking them and any other scrap metal they came across to collection places, where periodically they would be gathered, shipped to smelters, and transformed into guns and army tanks. People saved bacon grease and took it to depositories where it was collected and transformed into explosives. That was the word that Franklin Roosevelt put out, at any rate. Tires were rationed, as was sugar, coffee, gasoline, and many other things. Some things were simply not available at all, such as butter— hence the development of oleomargarine. Margarine came with packets of powdered orange color. The dyes were provided for mixing so that the pale mass of white grease could be made to resemble butter. There was no bubble gum. No rubber balloons. World War II was raging, on and on, and while American boys were falling dead on foreign battlefields far away, Andy Prather, David Kinard, and I were filling these wonderful new discoveries I had found in my parents' dresser drawer with natural gas and floating them high above the neighborhood. These were sparkling, transparent blimps of latex, silently obeying the law of gaseous buoyancy.

Andy and David knew what they were, and what they were used for. Me? I did not have a clue. They told me, but I still had little comprehension. To me they were simply works of art, mystery, and beauty. They sparkled, and the substance they were designed to retain had always been a verb and never a noun. I was completely confused.

There is no way for me to know how many shocked little old ladies watched in both horror and fantasy from their quiet parlor windows as our fleet of "Sheiks" sailed by them, high in the Colorado City, Texas, sky.

Alas! Nothing lasts forever, especially a box of latex prophylactics. Demand reduced the supply until there were no more. As with many other items, rubber balloons were not available because it was wartime. American industrial energies went into the manufacture of planes, ships, tanks, Jeeps, and munitions—not into toys and sundries. Our "Royal Air Force Blimp Corps" became obsolete, defunct. So with our supply of "balloons" completely depleted, we directed our energies toward other pursuits.

I learned several things from this experience. I learned that natural gas is lighter than the earth's immediate atmosphere. I learned that mercaptan smells very bad. I learned that although shooting at floating condoms is great sport, they are difficult to hit with artillery limited to slingshots. I learned that what goes up comes down, be it a condom or a stone launched from a propelling device, and such can come down in very unexpected places—like through the Wallace's front window and onto their living room floor, shattering glass in the process.

I learned also that when the libido of the man of the house commands him to perform, and he abruptly becomes aware that he has no condoms, his emotional state greatly resembles that of an angry Hebrew God. In the book of Exodus, God tells Moses that he may not see His face and live. When my father awakened me at daylight, and in a state of great wrath said, "You and Andy Prather stole balloons from my drawer!" I looked upon his face and knew I was a goner. Me? I was one fallen angel. He told me he was going to punish me worse than I had ever been punished, adding that when murderers are on death row, they are often given years to contemplate their wrongdoings. He told me he did not know for certain when he was going to punish me, but that he was going to punish me. I lived in terror for a long time. After two years or so, I thought he had probably forgotten about it. He died some forty years later. We made peace about many things before he did.

I'll tell you one thing: growing up can be a really hard experience! I will tell you another thing: I broke the cycle. I have never one time abused a child.

RIGHT: WORRELL'S FIRST PAINTING, *"NIPPLE PEAK"* – OIL, 8" X 10." CIRCA 1956.

XXXIV.
NIPPLE PEAK

PERSONALITIES ARE ENERGIES. They always have an effect upon us. At least they do if we associate with them. Sometimes they do even if we do not associate with them! These effects endure for life, even if they somehow dwell within the subconscious. These personalities, these energies, can be negative or they can be positive. The energy of Charles Henry Lane, D. C. was and is incredibly positive.

I was fourteen. He was eighty. We were best friends. He was an "old-fashioned" chiropractor. I was a green and naive hayseed freshman kid, just beginning high school. Doc Lane did not own a car. I had a 1939 Chevrolet sedan. It was actually my parents' car, but they let me use it, and in those days one could possess a Texas driver's license at age fourteen.

On various and random Sunday mornings, usually at 4:30 or 5:00 a.m., I would drive to his downtown upstairs office. He called it a clinic. It was on Main Street in Colorado City, Texas. I would fetch him, and we would drive to Silver or Robert Lee on 19.9¢ per gallon gasoline. There we would get coffee in some open-all-night oil field cafe. Bitter coffee, it was. Not gourmet by any stretch of any fantasy. It was two notches below lobby coffee provided by some cheap motel. It took a while, but I learned to drink it and also to like it.

We drank early morning coffee, and during times of ten more cents worth of prosperity, we might have a doughnut to go with it—a sweet, greasy doughnut. Stale, perhaps, but good. We would be thus engaged while waiting for sunrise and imagining corner tang knives, oval blades, Folsom points, and all kinds of flaked flint wonders.

We would be on the banks of the Colorado River by gray dawning light. Back then those ancient prehistoric campsites seemed endless. There were thousands, even millions, of flint chips—leftovers strewn atop and among midden mounds: products, by-products, and even debris of the toolmakers' arts.

The old man carried a little three-pronged garden rake and a flour sack containing a quart Mason jar of water. Along with these he would have a piece of fruit. With his flour sack and rake, he would pass the hours walking and searching in the drought-ridden hot afternoons, turning over and turning up pieces of flint. The old man's eyes were keen, and he usually found many more artifacts than I did.

The dead of long ago walked these hills, valleys, and beside these streams. Their spirits still do. If one is still, quiet, reverent, and in a proper attitude, then one will feel their presence and their energy. The scoffers, of course, are seldom still, quiet, reverent, or in the proper attitude, so they never feel the presence of the ancient spirits and simply ridicule those who do or scoff at those who say they do.

I walked those haunts with Doc Lane over fifty years ago and

sometimes with Doc and David (Clabber) Merritt. This was often at
a place called Nipple Peak. It was my most favorite of all places to go
to hunt arrowheads, as we called them. My first oil painting was of
Nipple Peak, done from memory while I was a student at Texas Tech.
It is really a poor painting, for I knew little about color harmony, value,
composition, rendering perspective, or other fundamental elements of
painting. I still have that little 8 x 10 rendering. In my dreams I still
dream about roaming around Nipple Peak.

I carried a small triangular hoe and a leg from an old pair of
Levis knotted in the sheared end. This formed a rather nice bag, and I
would bring it home filled with scrapers and tools, along with broken
knives and points.

"Hunting arrowheads" is what we called it, and in my blissful
ignorance I envisioned the flint artifacts being made during days just
a bit before the times of our cowboy movie heroes. Our scant surface
finds did little to damage the scientific community; little did I know
then, when finding some flint points, it was likely they had not been
touched by human hands for two to seven thousand years. Many of
those artifacts lay there covered and then uncovered by the sands of
time; this happening while Moses led the children of Israel out of
Egyptian bondage. They lay there when Ezekiel lamented. They lay there
when Jesus hung upon a cross. They lay there during the Dark Ages
and as Magellan sailed the seas. They lay there when the conquistadors
enslaved the people of the great Southwest, and they lay there in silent
obscurity when I was born. They were there until I touched them, picked
them up, and felt their magic radiate into my being.

The old man was a major influence in my life.

The old man is gone
But his memory is strong
Lingers on in my mind
In the hills
And on the back roads

He only had a home for a little while
Then she told him they were through

And she left him
For some reason
He never knew

Doc lived a rather lonely life. He managed to hold on to his son when his wife left him, and they lived together in the old upstairs office on Main Street. This was both home and chiropractic clinic. We called his son, who was also named Charles, "T.D." We called him that because he played trombone as well as—or perhaps better—than Tommy Dorsey.

Doc feared his ex would slip back and take the son away, so every afternoon he would walk to the Coleman School and, hand in hand, they would stroll back to the upstairs office where a sign hung above the sidewalk. It read:

DR. CHARLES HENRY LANE, D.C.

Small towns and early morning cafes
And the old man with a longing in his eyes
Drinking black coffee
And waiting
For the sunrise

Burned out fields
And thirsty crops of cotton and maize
Cloudless skies
Hot summer haze
West Texas days

Down these still, dusty roads
I remember
Turning windmills with my hands
To get a drink from the land
For the old man,
Charles Henry Lane, D. C.

It never rained in the '50s in Mitchell or Coke Counties. At least it seemed that it never rained. Farming and ranching were dormant. Oil and gas sustained what local economy there was. Even this slumped in the '60s, and T.D. left Colorado City for Oregon to obtain work. By then Doc was in his nineties and had little choice other than tagging along. He came back to visit one time, and Clabber and I— once again, and for the last time— took the old man arrowhead hunting. It was our last trip together. I never saw him again, but I remember. I still have energy from him. I remember climbing a windmill tower on Bill Martin's ranch south of Robert Lee on a very hot and windless day. I spun the fan as Clabber pushed and pulled on the sucker rod. I remember the clear, cool liquid crystal that flowed from the pipe, and I remember the thirsty old man gratefully drinking. We drank, too.

Forget? Never! I remember Charles Henry Lane, D.C., and I remember Nipple Peak.

PHOTOGRAPH TAKEN 04/17/13.
VIEW FROM DISTANT HIGHWAY 208.

THE CLIFFS OF STEP MOUNTAIN.

XXXV.
STEP MOUNTAIN

STEP MOUNTAIN is practically right on the Mitchell County/Coke County line. It looks about the same today as I remember it looking back in 1952 when I first climbed it. It has been a place that has drawn me back many times. Here is how its cliffs appeared on April 18, 2013. I am in this photograph, above the beginning of the cliffs, almost in the center of the image. So is my early day friend Hollis Gainey.

Someone might have labeled me accurately by stating I was a Texas Aborigine. I was at least seven-eighths wild, and the other one-eighth needed considerable grooming. I would do almost anything to escape captivity inside the city limits.

WE ARE A LONG WAY UP.

KIX BROOKS: THE LEDGE WAS
BAD ENOUGH. THE CACTUS
COMPOUNDED THE DIFFICULTY.

KIX AND ERIC PUTTING IN THE
REPLACEMENT LETTER.

Nightfall might find me making my way back to the car from some ancient American Indian campsite where I had been searching for flint artifacts since dawn. It might find me in some rowboat still chunking plugs for black bass. It might find me out in the shinnery sands playing around on the dunes. It often found me camped on top of Step Mountain, twenty-six miles south of Colorado City and a couple of miles east of Silver. (Shinnery is a local colloquial word referring to a species of dwarf oak that only grows about shin high.)

Step Mountain was one of my favorite haunts; it had been since early high school. It was wild and remote, with prodigious limestone boulders and escarpments. In its cliffs were various fractures, some of which broke into long and narrow caves. Some of my friends and I were demented enough in those days to squeeze ourselves through various chambers of these, hoping we would not encounter a large diamondback—or a den of them. We also trusted that the earth would not shift and suddenly set a billion tons of ancient seabed reef upon us.

This place had a captivating energy for me, and I dearly loved being there. My dad went with me there one time, and together we scaled the rocks to the mesa top. We did this despite his almost 70 years and his severe World War I wounds and disabilities.

Step Mountain was not my only love. I loved a little country girl who lived in the east part of Mitchell County, over the other side of Loraine. I mean I really loved her! It was love, pure love, beyond any doubt. Some have but one love throughout life. "True love," they label it. "The love of my life" some call it. With whatever similarities, it probably varies with every person. I know I have been in love more than one time. I have probably also confused love with estrus, or the rut for that matter. The flames of passion can be misunderstood. They can be misinterpreted.

I did not misinterpret my feelings about her. It was not blind passion, and it was not simply the rut. It was as pure a feeling as ever a man has felt about a woman. Ah! She was too young. I was too, but I only know that now. As the old Sam Cooke song goes:

"She was only sixteen, just sixteen,

But oh how those two eyes could glow,
She was too young to fall in love,
And I was too young to know."

With each date my feelings grew deeper. I wanted to marry her
and live with her for the rest of my life. She consumed almost all of my
conscious thoughts. She lived near a small town about ten miles east of
Colorado City and was in high school at the time. I was in college at
Lubbock and that made the distance even greater: 110 miles.

It was 1956, as I recall. I was enrolled at Texas Technological
College (now known as Texas Tech University) when the postman
brought to my door yet another one of those sad things known as a
"Dear John Letter." I was stunned. I was sad beyond description. I felt
like the old Jack Greene country song,

"There goes my reason for living,
There goes my everything."

My dad and I were close in some ways, and in other ways we
were great distances apart. We were very close regarding golf, politics,
philosophy, astronomy, and such things as that, but our relationship was
not one that engendered having conversations about romantic breakups.
I had a similar relationship with my mother. I do not know why. I
wonder about this from time to time, wonder about the reasons why.
It was some sort of timidity or embarrassment I suppose. I just did not
have anyone to talk with about this situation other than my roommate,
and he really did not seem to understand it very well. There was no one
with whom to share my sorrow.

Despite the despair, I had faith. I had enough faith to think
that someday I would get over it, and things would be all right. So I
did something. Some might regard this as a bit unusual, but it was not
unusual for a hopeless romantic like I was. I sprayed that letter with
clear plastic, and I sprayed the envelope, too. I put a thick coat on both
of them. Then I went to Step Mountain, climbed the cliffs, walked a
ways on a narrow ledge part way up, and stuffed the envelope and letter
deep into a crack beneath the shelter of the rocks above. The last time I

looked, it was still there. That was about 1979, so it had been there for twenty-three years.

At the time I placed this sad, sad letter in the crack, I had conjured enough faith to believe I would heal from the wound, and that someday I might have a son suffering the same romantic heartache. If this should ever come to pass, I would take him to Step Mountain—to the cliffs, to the crack in the rocks. There we would find that letter, the "There goes my everything" note from a young country girl, read it together, and I would assure him that a broken heart is not the end of the world.

There is energy about that place called Step Mountain, and a bit of mystery, too. There is a flowing spring at the north end. It is named Jackson Springs and was an ancient Indian Camp. The cliffs of the mountain are less than a mile away—those cliffs where I would wager the letter is still where it has been for fifty-six years. I think I will go retrieve it, frame it, and hang it on my studio wall. Of course, I will replace it with another note that will simply state, "This is where the letter was."

FOOTNOTE: Fifty-seven years is less than the blinking of an eye in terms of geological time. It is a long time in terms of one human's experience. Did rodents get the letter? Did some human explorer find it and remove it? Was it yet there stuffed back into the depths of that crack eluding our sight? After our retrieval odyssey was over, I remembered about 1978, I took a long, thin stick and pushed the letter far back into the crack so no one would be apt to find it. Whatever is the case, we replaced it with a new one written September 11, 2013 and signed by me, Kix and Eric Brooks, and also signed by the base support group, Spider Johnson, Mike and Diana McCabe, Gay Houston, and Marti Perkins.

Eric will go back to that cave some day, maybe when he is age fifty, and take his son. Probably, as he is showing his son the letter we stuffed in the cave 25 years before, they will both discover the original that was so cleverly hiding from our view.

RIGHT: FLINT POINTS
FOUND AT NEW ART.

XXXVI.
HELL'S GATE

I WAS IN MY MID-TWENTIES when I became a district executive for the Boy Scouts of America. District Scout executives were given that illustrious title so we would not be confused with ditch diggers, employees of city street repair crews, custodians, or other blue-collar workers. We were really all of these, in addition to being organizers of Boy Scout troops, Cub Scout packs, and Explorer posts. The Circle Ten Council in Dallas, Texas, employed me, and I was paid the fantastic salary of $3,800 a year; that, and I received a Christmas bonus of $50.

I had many wonderful experiences as a professional Scouter, and I met many fine people. I was co-director of one of our camps at Mill

Creek on Lake Texoma. This afforded me the opportunity to do some things that were right up my alley: to go fishing a couple of times a day and to hunt arrowheads. The fishing was good, and there was an ancient Indian campsite that was inundated by the impounded waters a short canoe ride from the camp headquarters. I would take a screen strainer and sieve through the sand to find arrowheads and other flint artifacts. Doing that was very enjoyable, but I was too young and green to realize just how much fun it was at the time.

I learned a lot while working for the Boy Scouts of America. Much of what I learned was positive. Some of it was negative. I became a Cub Scout at age eight. As such I learned and avowed, "I, Bill Worrell, promise to do my best, to do my duty to God and my Country, to help other people, and to obey the law of the pack."

The law of the pack was that "the Cub Scout follows Akela. The Cub Scout helps the pack go. The pack helps the Cub Scout grow. The Cub Scout gives goodwill."

There was also a Cub Scout motto. It was (and is), "Do your best."

From Mrs. Bridgeford's Cub Scout den, I matriculated at age twelve into the Boy Scouts becoming a member of Troop 20, sponsored by the First Methodist Church of Colorado City, Texas. As a Boy Scout I took an oath: "On my honor I will do my best to do my duty to God and my country and to obey the Scout law; to help other people at all times; to keep myself physically strong, mentally awake, and morally straight."

There was also a law unto which I subscribed. It had twelve points. These were: "A Scout is trustworthy, loyal, helpful, friendly, courteous, kind, obedient, cheerful, thrifty, brave, clean, and reverent." I learned to "do a good turn daily" and to "be prepared," those being the Scout slogan and the Scout motto.

At age fourteen I became an explorer in a Sea Scout Ship. Imagine that in a West Texas town! There was no ocean and there was no sea, but we had a Sea Scout Ship! After I was graduated from Texas

XXXVI. *Hell's Gate*

Tech, I became a scoutmaster, and while a college professor, I was a merit badge counselor.

I was in for a shock working for the Boy Scouts of America. There were professional Scouters who turned the air blue at the Council office. They turned it blue with vulgar jokes and by using God's name in vain, along with other words considered vulgar and obscene. The demeanor around the council office seemed a lot like that around the refinery and the oil patch. "A Scout is reverent?" I thought.

Membership dues were fifty cents a year for a boy to belong to the Scouts. This was prorated so that if a unit charter was issued in January and a boy joined that unit in December, it only cost him five cents to join. This gave him membership until the end of January. Raises and advancement for professional Scouters were based upon membership growth. Come December, some of the district executives would go through the phone book and log in surnames then make up first names of "new enrollees." This cost them a nickel a name, which they paid out of their own pockets, but the raises they received for increased membership made that profitable. They would show a great drop in membership at the end of January, and come the next December they would have to fake even higher numbers. "A Scout is trustworthy?" I thought. What energy! What karma!

One day I entered the blue atmosphere of the lobby of the council office. The director of camping looked at me and said, "We are going to send you to the National Camping School—to the aquatics division." And I was sent. In those times I was somewhat of a water rat. I could swim like an otter and I loved the water. I did not know that my love for swimming would soon change.

It was May 1964. The BSA National Camping School was held at Possum Kingdom, a lake in Grayson County, Texas, near a place named Hell's Gate. Although the weather was mild, the water was extremely cold, and the wind blew incessantly. All except one of the staff members were ex-military personnel, and they pretended they were still in the Marines. They pretended we were trainees at boot camp. They did all within their power to make life miserable for us. They were successful, too.

Breakfast was at seven o'clock each morning, after which we were ordered to immediately gather in swimsuits on the T dock. "Okay! Hit the water!" That was the 8:00 a.m. order. We would be in the lake for about five minutes, just long enough to get accustomed to the chill, before we were ordered back onto the dock. Shivering, and with teeth chattering, we would lie flat on the wooden planks in attempts to get out of the never-ceasing wind. About the time we warmed up, it came again—the order to "hit the water."

This went on until noon; then we had a short break for lunch. We had about ten minutes afterward to engage in free time activities. Then it was back on the T dock. We swam, rowed, canoed, and life-saved until 5:00 p.m. when we were again given a short break before dinner. After dinner we immediately gathered on the T dock and engaged in aquatic activities until 9:00 p.m. Then we were released to our tents for the night. "A Scout is kind?" I thought.

There was one week of this hell near Hell's Gate. There was only one man who showed any kindness at all, and I respected him for that. I learned that he was later sent to prison for committing sodomy with a twelve-year-old boy on a camp out. "A Scout is clean and reverent?" I thought.

Some ten years later, I became the director of the aquatics section of this National Camping School. This was long after I had resigned as a professional Scouter and had become a college art teacher. I was involved in these camping schools for three or four years and then went on to other things. Not one time did I abuse another trainee, regardless of how refractory he might be to learning what we were charged to teach. Some of it was very trying. Some candidates could not even swim. Some were from Arizona Indian reservations and had never seen water deeper than what a glass or cup might hold. Some were almost devoid of coordination. But I learned something from all the bad energy and misused power of my own aquatics school experience. I learned to always try to treat others kindly. I might fail in this, but I attempt to keep it in mind whether the kindness is to human beings or animal beings.

I owe much to the Scouting program. It is one of the reasons I

222

FLINT ARTIFACTS FOUND IN MITCHELL
AND COKE COUNTIES.

am where I am today and doing what I have been successful in doing. As a boy, the *Handbook for Boys* was my main reading source. Every afternoon I read it just as soon as I got home from school. I made things, created things, crafted things, melted metal, and even cast it into molds I fashioned. I chipped arrowheads from flint I picked up at ancient Indian campsites. I tied knots with rope. I learned Morse Code. I became a painter and a sculptor. I remain grateful for the energy and the power that the Scouting program bestowed upon me, along with the memories of boyhood friends, hikes, camping trips, and the Scout Oath, Law, Motto, and Slogan. What a wonderful world it would be if everyone lived by these creeds. What a powerful energy that would be!

XXXVII.
OLD TIME RELIGION

> GIVE ME that old time religion
> Give me that old time religion
> Give me that old time religion
> It's good enough for me

So goes the old song that is sung in many fundamental church revival meetings. That "old time religion" has confused many a soul, including mine. It has especially confused the souls of tender, sensitive, young, naive, and gullible children. I think some of us remain children longer than others, and I think I was one of these. Way into my college days I was one of these. I perceived myself beneath the level of my classmates and peers. I thought they knew so much more than I knew!

Over a half-century later, I reflect about how incorrect I was. I can now fathom many clues about how much they relied upon me— upon my perceptions about life and about spirituality. Yet then, back in those dismal "dark ages," I felt so uncertain and so lost— not lost in New Testament terms, but rather, lost within a social order.

"Salad days" cannot begin to describe how green I was when I was in my twenties. I was as naïve as ever a person has been. I allowed myself to become infected with a not-so-healthy brand of organized religious philosophy and was "called to the ministry." Religion was my great escape from the more common frightening social order. That led me to becoming the pastor of a small rural Southern Baptist Congregation. It was the Fairview Baptist Church located near Cuthbert, Texas. Cuthbert was in the middle of nowhere and no longer even exists, except perhaps for a historical marker where the Raymond Uzzel General Store once stood. There is scarcely a structure that has not been razed: houses, the store, the schoolhouse, and the Fairview Church. Many were the days I would find myself in that lonely and remote building attempting to study the "Word" to gain some divine inspiration for a sermon. In retrospect, I believe "inspirations" came from erstwhile aspiration, perhaps an illusion of grandeur, perhaps from my old adversary—my ego—and not from Divine Providence. I tried to be a diligent, faithful, steadfast, hardworking witness for the Lord. The ministry led me into many a place of strange energy, I assure you! It led me into places of extremely uncomfortable prayers and grossly repulsive lunches and dinners. I will omit the details lest I cause you to develop emesis. It led me to visitations with church members who had chickens living in their houses. It led me to scenes of strange hand-holdings and hand shakings. It led into hugging, clinging, sobbing confessions I did not care to hear.

One time that old time religion led me down a labyrinth of remote unpaved roads to a desolate place beside the Colorado River, the Chainey's trailer house. The Chainey's trailer house! What an experience! I do not remember his name, but God knows I remember that dog! The Chainey's dog. If I live two hundred years, I will not forget the monstrous, barking, foaming-at-the-mouth, leg biting Chainey's dog! My paranoia made me think the family was inside the trailer house laughing at me because I was scared to get out of my car. Both my ego and my conviction to witness for the Lord made me get out. This caused me to be attacked by the dog.

Remember, I was green. Really green. I was still just a hayseed kid. A kid from a small town in the Permian Basin named Colorado City, Texas. I think its 5,000-population figure was Chamber of Commerce tabulation and included dogs, cats, and parakeets. It was deep in the West Texas Bible belt. It had a history of farming, ranching, oil, sin and salvation. It has long been called the "Mother City of West Texas" because it was the only stopping place with "modern conveniences" between Fort Worth and El Paso.

People who were "not from there" self-righteously mispronounced the town's name in a way similar to how they most generally mispronounce the name of the state of Colorado. The locals simply, and in typical West Texas style, mispronounced it as "Kaul-uh-ray-duh."

Fort Worth is 215 miles to the east and El Paso almost 400 miles to the west. This made Colorado City a favored oasis. There was Jake's Hotel and the Opera House, if nothing much more than those. There were also several saloons in the early days, but by the thirties the only booze to be found was well hidden in the closets of discreet churchgoers or at the bootleggers. The bootleggers were in "the sands" and on the "south side." There was a country club with a nine-hole "sand-green" golf course and slot machines. That was a place where beer and spirits freely flowed. There was also plenty of everything over at Big Spring, forty miles west on Highway 80. Many a Colorado City resident was to be found on the highway either going to or coming from the Big Spring oasis. Some of the churchgoers could also be found dancing in Big Spring. Dancing, of all sinful things: dancing to the music of Hoyle Nix and his West Texas Playboys at the Stampede. Hoyle wrote the classic "Big Balls in Cowtown," and people went hog wild when he played it. Colorado City was as much a Peyton Place as any other small

town has ever been, even though it attempted to be the buckle on the
Bible belt.

I was reared Methodist, later defecting to the Southern Baptists.
Very few Baptists in Colorado City drank in front of one another, and
the Methodists there were stronger teetotalers than Carrie Nation, who
limited her pleasurable libations to opium tea. Everyone who did not
belong to The Church of Christ was going to hell, to burn forever. The
Assembly of God members were referred to as "Holy Rollers." There
were Episcopalians, but not many. Their church building is a historically
marked place. Most Catholics were Hispanic, and the Catholic
Church was in the sands. This imposed a rather unique integration
upon Anglos and Hispanics. There were various other religious sects:
Nazarenes, Adventists, Presbyterians, a few Lutherans, and several
small fundamentalist groups. Both the churches and the schools were
segregated, except for the Catholic Church.

As the troublesome middle child, I was quite a hell raiser until
I walked the aisle and got "saved." This salvation almost killed me, and
that gets us back to the Fairview Baptist Church.

Eunice McMillan was a deacon. He and his wife, Versie, were
stalwarts of the membership, and they were wonderful, kind human
beings. One day, Eunice told me a new family had moved into the
community. Their name was Chainey. He told me we should pay them a
visit and invite them to church. That is what we did.

The Chaineys were oil field people and lived off a paved farm-
to-market road, down an unpaved county road, then through a gap onto
a dirt lane that led to the north side of The Colorado River. There, in the
middle of nowhere, rested the Chainey's trailer house. Except for the
trailer house part, it was my kind of place because it was wild pasture on
an ancient Indian campsite and very remote.

When we pulled up in my green 1957 Oldsmobile, the largest
German Shepherd I had ever seen greeted us. He was also the most
vicious I have ever encountered. His fur was upright hackle. His fangs
were bared, and white foam sprayed from his barking, growling mouth,
splashing to the ground in wet pools.

As Mr. McMillan and I looked at one another in astonishment and disbelief, Mrs. Chainey opened the door and called to the dog. "Killer!!! Stay!!!" He did—pacing in tight circles—looking at us with a keen appetite from his piercing eyes, while his mouth watered through his dagger-like teeth, and the foam drooled to the ground.

Mrs. Chainey was a pleasant and friendly woman. She explained that they had moved to Mitchell County from Odessa where her husband had been employed by an oil field company. Someone had given them the dog, and they just could not seem to get him settled down—although being so far out in the country, she felt safe with him around.

To our delight, the Chaineys came to evening worship services the following Sunday, and they even stayed around afterward visiting and talking for a while, as is the custom in many small rural congregations. They did not come again, however, and after a few weeks I decided that I should pay them another visit. Eunice was not to be found. Neither was T.J. Geiger, another deacon, so I went alone.

Over the years I have wondered about and questioned both my wisdom and my motivation for going back there. My questions have been: Was God telling me to do this? Was guilt prompting me? Was it that old time religion, the customary thing to do? Was it that old and ancient foe of mine, the ego? Whoever or whichever, I once again found myself driving down the lonesome dirt lane and parking in front of the trailer. The dog was at home! Once again he looked into the window, teeth bared, hackle standing upright, white slobber pouring from his huge mouth, and he barked loudly between menacing growls. There were two or three cars parked near the trailer house, so I presumed someone was at home and that, any minute, Mrs. Chainey would appear at the door and call the animal off.

That did not happen. I sat in my car creating novels. I created novels about how preachers are the brunt of so many jokes and about how people were probably looking out the windows and seeing a "man of God" in fear. I could imagine them laughing at a cowardly preacher, one afraid of a barking dog. If they were, they were correct, for I was scared as the vernacular!

I sat there wondering what to do. If I did not go to the door, I would forever "lose my witness" with these people and never get them back to church again. If I went to the door, I would probably soon resemble hamburger meat. Well, Peter got out of the boat in the sea, and I got out of the car. Peter walked on the water, and I walked to the door, some sixty or seventy feet away. Peter sank after a few steps. I figured I was about to sink too! I knew that son of a bitch (literally stated) would likely first go for one of my wrists. In this case it would be crushed, and I would never be the artist I wanted to be. It then flashed through my mind just how moot this point was because I was soon going to be dead anyway. Also flashing through my mind was the story about the recent incident nearby where two German Shepherds had attacked and killed a woman.

As I made my way to the trailer, I pretended to stretch and yawn, holding my hands above my head, ready to defend my throat and also protect my wrists and fingers from the canine's crushing jaws.

"God in Heaven let someone be at home! Please!" It was an unnecessary prayer. It was a prayer as stupid as asking the Lord to make Dallas the capital of Texas just to accommodate a wrong answer on a geography test. I was in this dog's kingdom, and he wanted a piece of me. I stepped up on the porch. Behold, I stood at the door and knocked! Knock-knock-knock!!! Behold, I waited and there was no reply. Knock-knock-knock!!! And again I knocked. I knew I was a goner. My heart was pounding too hard to hear God speaking to me, but if I could have heard Him, the words spoken would have probably been:

"Now Worrell, why did you do such a stupid thing? Don't you remember what I wrote in my Book about pride?"

I opened the long blade of my Case knife while sadly thinking that if I killed this dog, I would never get these folks back to church again. I offered my left hand as the first and easiest target—thinking I could jab out both his eyes while he was crushing the hand to bits. Then I would go for the throat. I was regretting losing my witness with these people as I descended the first step. The dog charged, growling and biting my right gluteus. As he did, I screamed at him as loudly as I could, "HEAYAAW!" Then I kept my front toward him and my eyes staring into his. This startled him momentarily, and I backed toward the Oldsmobile.

I was green, but I was not completely stupid. The passenger door was closest to the trailer, and I had made my exit through it. Peter left the boat and walked on the water toward Jesus. I had left the car with whatever faith, and I had left the door wide open just in case something like this were to happen. "Be prepared," I remembered. Peter lost his faith and sank into the sea. I was wishing for a hole to sink into and was wondering why, in either God's name or hell, I had decided to visit the Chaineys.

I kept backing away from the German shepherd. He remained startled, standing his ground, barking, bristling, and foaming through his bared teeth. When I felt I could beat him to the car, I turned and sprinted for the open door, folding the knife blade against my thigh as I did so. I dived into the vehicle, pulling the door closed. I sat there with a pounding, racing heart, breathing heavily and watching the Chainey's dog look into my window. He was still barking, growling, and foaming at the mouth.

I drove away feeling an amalgamation of emotions: gratitude, stupidity, fear, and relief. Fifty years have gone by since this happened, and since then I have given every dog due respect and the benefit of all doubt.

I told Brother Geiger about the incident, and he just laughed as if he thought I was exaggerating. I drove him over to the Chainey's, and he quit laughing. The dog was barking when we pulled up. No one came to the door, and the dog was barking as we drove away. I never saw the Chaineys again.

Forty-five years after the dog attack, I drove back to the Fairview Church. It was gone. I could not find the well we had dug. The trees and shrubs we had planted were gone. The brick structure I had so carefully laid and the sign I had made were both gone. I had poured a concrete foundation, constructed a tier of red bricks, and carefully placed upon it letters reading: Fairview Church. Then I inscribed a passage of scripture into the concrete: "Except the Lord build a house, they labor in

BRICK FROM THE FAIRVIEW CHURCH SIGN.

vain that build it."

The hymns, funerals, weddings, prayers, revival meetings, and socializing that occurred at the Fairview Baptist Church bring memories of strange energies in a place that had some power and probably a good bit of mystery. I cannot honestly state that the energy was good energy. It must be true that except the Lord build the house, they labor in vain that build it, for there is not a trace of it remaining other than a few old red bricks scattered around. I picked one up and brought it back to my studio. It rests upon a shelf with this account briefly inscribed on it.

The Lord God knows how I wonder and wonder what ever happened to the people of that congregation, to the old men, the old women, the young boys and girls, and the people of the Cuthbert community. Perhaps it is what happened to the sign I made, to the trees planted, to the vines and flowers planted, to the well drilled, to the walls painted, to the floors sanded and varnished, to the steeple erected, and to all else that happened at the Fairview Church. As I wonder what happened to those things, to those fine people, to their young children who must be in their 60s now, to the good times of fellowship and the happenings of the Fairview Baptist Church, I read the first few verses of Ecclesiastes and I know the answer. Energy just dissipates into the universe and is scattered into the ether. All is forgotten. Then, all that was is no more. Maybe.

THE GLEN MARSHALL-MADE KNIFE
MY SON "MISPLACED"

XXXVIII.
LOST AND FOUND

MY SON RECENTLY TOLD ME, "I've never lost anything. It is just misplaced."

I have more than a fair share of misplaced things. These range from ancient artifacts to knives, firearms, old coins, tools, writings, photographs, tweezers, scissors, shampoo, CDs, letters, pens, telephones, sketchbooks, journals, paint brushes, tubes of paint, watercolor paper, cups of hot coffee, opened bottles of cold beer, fishing gear, jewelry, bananas & avocados, Fritos, flashlights, batteries, and perhaps even relationships. Eyeglasses are a major misplaced item! I have not lost anything; I have just misplaced things. Thinking about it as I type this,

I probably engaged in misplaced relationships, too! I am grateful now that some of them went south! Practically everything seems to surface with the passing of time, including flat beers, cold coffee, hard and black bananas, dehydrated avocados, and now and then an ex-girlfriend whom I have not seen in years.

Things have energies about them, and they can produce mysteries also. Some things remain misplaced much longer than other things, and of course other people have misplaced some of my things. I found a camera in the deep freeze one time after a new house cleaner had tidied things up. It took a long time to relocate it. It took longer to relocate some other items. This house cleaner won the international toilet bowl brush hiding championship. Recently, I found a missing pressure cooker still containing food and with a dirty bowl and a dirty spoon in it. Some guest had placed these in the cupboard. This was quite an odoriferous experience.

I found the bananas and avocados I misplaced—in my Suburban behind the seat and under a bedroll. They were mummified. The Fritos were in a camouflaged brown bag under the rear seat. I mistakenly thought that baking them in the oven would remove the stale taste. Two days ago I found a check for over $900 that had been hiding in a cardboard box for over a year. I located another one for $800 just as the flames devoured it in the wood stove. I have yet to relocate most of the misplaced relationships.

There can be a strange sort of energy when something lost is found or relocated. It is a bit like reconnecting with an old friend. Sometime in the early 1990s, my son and his business partner poured a concrete slab for me. The slab remained a lonesome concrete monolith over on the north side of the road until some five years later when I constructed a storage shed upon it. This was so designed as to later become a guesthouse or cabin. For some six or seven years, I used the shed to store shipping boxes and crating material then decided to move on with the guest house which was completed about 2007.

My son lost a very fine custom-crafted Glenn Marshall knife during the process of pouring the slab. I had given this to him as a present. He believed the knife was encased under the mass of concrete.

From time to time he would mention it, sort of lamenting the loss. On May 16, 2006, my horticulturist friend, Gay Ainsworth Houston, was helping me work flowerbeds and plant tomatoes, peppers, basil, and other things in these beds. You already know what she unearthed. It was the knife! The blade is stainless steel and the handle is lignum vitae; thus, there are a few discolored spots on the metal, and the handle is slightly cracked, but both can be restored to an almost like-new state. For some sixteen to eighteen years, this instrument lay beneath the soil, oftentimes just a few inches from my sight.

I photographed it, sent the photos to Billy, and asked him if he still had the sheath. He responded, "I know I do somewhere, I just don't know where. I've never really lost anything. It's just been misplaced."

Another interesting lost and found thing concerns a piece of jewelry that was created especially for me. Eric Mandeville was one of the best students I had in more than eighteen years of college and university teaching. There were a handful of others that excelled, but none quite like Eric. He was a psychology major at Houston Baptist University. He took my ceramics class as an elective. He quickly changed his major, graduated from HBU with a degree in art, and then earned a Masters of Fine Arts degree at a New York University.

Eric was a drummer, as I recall, and he would skip around the lab pounding on various items with clay-working tools. As he did so, he would have that strange look upon his countenance that drummers generally seem to have. He excelled in using the potter's wheel, and his hand-built pieces were extraordinary. He did equally well in the area of sculpture and created many interesting pieces by the lost wax casting method. While still an undergraduate, Eric had an article published in *Ceramics Monthly Magazine*. He had other things published as well, but I do not remember what they were.

One day Eric gave me a present. It was a small deer skull pendant inspired by some clay pieces I had created. I did not regard this as plagiarism. It was his statement of admiration for my work, and I wore it graciously. This was probably about 1984 or 1985; I do not recall for certain, but it was sometime before I left HBU in 1989. I was wearing it around New Art one day and suddenly noticed it was gone.

The cord had come untied, and the silver piece was lost. I looked for it around the campfire down in the campground by the Llano River. I did not find it. That was the logical place to look because that was where I made the discovery it was gone. Over the years I searched for it a little with no positive results.

On June 19, 2009, I was moving a water hose in the campground when something caught my eye. It was a bright piece of metal in the sand of a gopher mound. Instantly, I thought it was a lost gopher trap or perhaps a carelessly tossed ring tab. I was astounded to pick up the silver deer skull that Eric had made and given me—the one lost for probably over twenty-four years. It did not have a luster polish, but it was bright as it could be.

I think about this pendant with fascination. Through hot summers and cold winters, and through flood after flood after flood, it had been lying around in my campground. Sometimes it was covered by at least six feet of floodwater. How some gopher managed to dig it up—and then for me to find it—is a mystery. It is also a mystery it was not tarnished and blackened by the passing of time the way silver so often is.

Finding this pendant produced a bit of strange energy. It was a high. Euphoria. It was a bit like locating an old lost friend. The feeling it generated was a bit like the feeling I experience when I find some ancient piece of flint that was chipped, flaked, and knapped into a beautiful projectile point by some artisan centuries ago. It was another one of those awesome experiences.

THE SILVER PENDANT—LOST FOR ALMOST 25 YEARS.

XXXIX.
THE ENERGIES OF PERSONALITIES

SOME TWENTY-FIVE YEARS AGO, I had a friend I will refer to as Todd. In the early days of construction at New Art, he would come from Lubbock, a town 300 miles away, and he would camp here and help me with things such as hanging rafters for the shed attached to Medium Cotton. I was always grateful for his assistance, especially when I was doing tasks that are not easily performed by one person.

I liked Todd. I genuinely did. Yet I found him very difficult to be around. There was something about his personality that simply sapped my energies, and sapped them very quickly. I would find myself becoming depressed when I was around him, depressed and at a creative lull. Among our circle of friends, there were others who experienced the same negative energy from his aura, his demeanor. None of us knew what it was.

I have no idea whatever happened to him. I reached a point where I could not be around him, so I just ceased my contact with him. I did not shoo him away. I just placed distance between us. His energy was a siphon to my stores of creativity.

I have known other personalities that affected me like this, and I have known some, such as Doc Lane and Buckminster Fuller, who were so uplifting that I do not have words to describe the positive energy they radiated upon me. I am convinced that human personalities have auras and energies that influence and affect those around them. Sometimes I shudder when I wonder how I might be affecting others.

There was another interesting personality I knew. She was so comely she would make Venus pout with envy. Nothing more need be stated than that. She had a most charming personality. She was a talented actress, a comedian, and she could mesmerize the crowds at the Santa Fe clubs. We both had a bit of a crush on each other. I know because we both acknowledged this to each other, even though we did nothing to cultivate it, nurture it, and allow it to grow. Ah! But she was so restless, so unsettled, and so uncertain as to who she was, what she wanted, and what she wanted to be. She seemed to continuously create an aura and an uncertainty and then amalgamate it into her persona.

People do create energies. That is what a personality is; it is energy. Some of these energies are so clean, wholesome and pure, and so refreshing to be around. Some are so negative that they are like vacuums or black holes that rob and steal and suck everything out of those around them, including positive attitudes and the perception of the joy of life. She did not seem to be this way at all, but she wore a mask, I think. It was one that concealed her misery and allowed her to hide her tormented state of mind.

Sometime a year or two before I met her, she had driven from

New Jersey to Santa Fe to have an adventure. Like so many other adventurers have done, she fell in love with the village and the area and made it her home.

Who but God can know what possessed her: A demon? Anger so deep it prodded her to get even with somebody, with anybody, or with everybody for anything and everything that had ever troubled or tormented her?

One day she left Santa Fe and drove to Taos, then west from there towards Tres Piedras, stopping at the Rio Grande Gorge Bridge. This is a spectacular place, and the bridge that spans the Rio Grande River six hundred feet below is an engineering marvel. Thousands of people visit this marvelous canyon. There are aisles on either side of the bridge for tourists to walk and view the rapids below while feasting upon the vastness of the surrounding terrain. In times past, I have dropped rocks and coins from this bridge and timed their falls: 32 feet the first second, 64 feet the next second, 96.5 feet the next second, until a maximum velocity of 321.7 feet per second is reached. That is really fast. Three hundred feet is the length of a football field.

I wonder what she thought as she was falling. Was it regret that she had jumped? Was it, "I'll get even?" Was it, "I'll show them?" Was it, "They'll be so sad?" Was it, "This is taking a lot longer than I thought?" She fell between six and seven seconds, and then she entered into her next realm of forever. Perhaps her soul is now one of those restless spirits that haunts the rushing waters and the canyons of the Rio Grande River.

THE OLD MOTEL UNIT AT THE EAGLE NEST
LODGE. SKETCH CIRCA 1974.

RIGHT: THE EAGLE NEST LODGE SIGN.

XL.
THE EAGLE NEST LODGE

I MET WALTER GANT IN 1971 when I was dating his granddaughter, Gilda Gant. Walter lived in Ardmore, Oklahoma. He was an oilman, a horseman, holder of vast lands in various places, and he was what is colloquially referred to as "a horse trader." Walter always did things his way. He had two sons, Cecil and Jack. Both worked for Walter, and to my knowledge that is all they ever did in the way of holding employment.

Walter owned the largest gated horse farm in America, or so he said, and so his family said. It was near Ardmore. There were vast stables, so many horses I couldn't count them, and mountains of baling wire that had grown higher and higher over the decades as they were discarded from the straw that they bound. He loved his horses, and to keep them in feed, he would sell land and holdings.

Among his land holdings were several thousand acres in northeastern New Mexico, an area east of Taos and southeast of Red River. The Dr. Pepper Company had propositioned Mr. Gant to build a lodge at Therma, New Mexico, and lease it to the company for recreational purposes. He did this and named it the Eagle Nest Lodge. It was quite fashionable. That is, it was quite fashionable in its quaint and rustic manner. It hosted various dignitaries such as the families of Alexander Graham Bell and the Grosvenors of *National Geographic Magazine*. It was such a well-known place that Therma changed the town name to Eagle Nest, New Mexico. The Springer Land and Cattle Company constructed a dam on the Cimarron River and named it Eagle Nest Lake. It was one of the best trout-fishing lakes in the country. It was privately owned by the Springer outfit, and fishing it was a sport for the wealthy and elite.

Walter Gant's elder son, Cecil, was placed in charge of the lodge along with the younger son, Jack, and his new bride, Evelyn. The great depression and its aftermath probably affected the Eagle Nest Lodge, and it folded. Its former glories became memories. The pride of Northern New Mexico became a white elephant. Gant was a frugal man, to state it laconically, and many corners had been cut during the construction of the lodge. This rendered its upkeep a very challenging thing.

December 28, 1971, was the fateful evening when I married Walter Gant's granddaughter. That was likely two of the largest mistakes two people ever made. But God is merciful, and He has a way of allowing good things to emerge out of strife and chaos.

Gilda and I would go to the Eagle Nest Lodge a couple of times a year; sometimes we would spend most of the summer there. We would host some of our friends from Texas for a few days at a time, and we would always bring my daughter, Sawndra, and my son, Billy, to vacation after they finished with Little League baseball and cheerleading camps.

The lodge was essentially a ruin by then, and it had the ambience of an ancient one to me. The lounge and the bar were pretty creepy. There were cobwebs, and there were molding and flaking items of taxidermy hanging on the walls and resting on tables and stands. These would seem to stare at us in silent reproach as if we had been the ones to shoot them, stuff them, and place them there. There were water stains and rotting floors from leaks in the roof. A sign was still hanging by the bar: "Welcome to the Loafer's Lounge."

There was an upright piano in the dining room, and it was amazingly still mostly in tune. There was a very large oil-burning range in the kitchen. It was very difficult to light, so we were instructed to keep it burning all the time. That did not require too much money back in those days when petroleum products were not so expensive. Behind the kitchen was a servant's room.

There was a reception booth, or check-in and check-out station, in the front hallway. Above this was a sign that both welcomed guests to enjoy their stay at the Eagle Nest Lodge and admonished them to pick up after themselves so the operators and employees could enjoy the place also.

There were mouse and rat droppings in great abundance. My second commanded task upon arrival was that I sweep them up and dispose of them. My first ordered task was to get the plumbing operable and the water running. Due to the very severe winters in northeastern New Mexico, this was an ordeal of multiple tasking, for there were always broken pipes needing repair. There were commodes to service, water heaters to light, and invariably, there were drowned mice in the reservoir. The reservoir was a small covered pit adjacent to the well out front. Water was pumped into the pit and then from the pit into the lodge. This made little sense to me, but that was the way it was. Mice would fall into the pit, were unable to get out, and would drown. The chilly water preserved them. After fishing them out, I would run water through all the pipes for an hour or so to "get the mouse out of them" before I would allow anyone to drink from the taps. Even after this ordeal, I still had a difficult time with it and preferred beer to water from that reservoir.

At that time my son was a very clever, inventive, and ingenuous ten-year-old boy. I do not know how many different live traps he invented and devised, but he caught numerous rodents which he always released out on the grounds. There seemed to be no shortage of mice, and this kept him entertained.

One of the saddening things about the rodents was the numerous gnawed and shredded Navajo and Hopi weavings, weavings that had once beautifully graced the inside of the lodge. These were priceless antiques of a bygone era, and they were unfortunately recycled into vermin nests.

There was an upstairs bath and a few guest bedrooms. Like everything else about the place, they were in very bad repair. The elevation at Eagle Nest is over 8,000 feet, so it is way too cold for roaches—at least we did not encounter any. There were a few ants, as it seems there always are, and there were flies and mosquitoes, but that was about it.

There was a caretaker's house some thirty yards to the east of the main structure. Cecil lived in that space, which was little better than the lodge. He kept a light bulb burning by the front entrance twenty-four/seven. It had no shade or covering, and it was always on, day and night.

Cecil was a jolly and friendly man known by everyone in the township of Eagle Nest where he went daily to get the paper, drink coffee, and to visit. Other than that, he did nothing, nothing other than to draw a bit and write letters. He was very skilled at drawing and coloring although he made no attempts to market his work. Jack and Evelyn had long ago moved back to Ardmore, and Cecil lived alone. He and his wife had divorced years before he took residence at the lodge. They had a son who was later struck and killed by lightening on a lake near Ardmore. Cecil did not keep the place up very well. I think this was partly because he did not have the energy for it and mostly because Walter would not allocate the needed funds for him to do so. Walter doled out an allowance to him for keeping an eye on the place, although this did not deter vandals from stealing the one-armed bandits and other items from the gaming room.

My children loved their stepmother, Gilda Gant. About the only good thing in our marriage was that she in turn loved them. Past that, we had little in common.

In later years I learned how frightened my kids were in that old lodge. There was energy about the place, and honestly it was a bit mysterious and spooky, yet there was pleasantness in being there, especially when friends would join us for a few days. I also later learned that the Eagle Nest Lodge gave some of them the willies and the creeps, too. The only times I became uneasy were when I would read fear in them. Other than their uneasiness, nothing there bothered me. I would often walk about the place in hours of darkness. I would sometimes venture into the dim basement that was filled with junk and clutter. I would look about in awe and wonder how anyone could create such a mess or why anyone would store such junk that had no use at all except to occupy space. But there was a small motel unit west of the lodge I only entered in daylight hours. I do not know why this was, but nighttime made it quite foreboding. It was an extremely lonely place, and it seemed that it might have the ghosts of many old memories penned within its walls.

The Eagle Nest Lodge had strong energy of bygone days, days of the 1930s and 1940s. Those were the days of Georgia O'Keeffe, Mabel Dodge Lujan, Roy Rogers and Dale Evans, Gene Autry, and the likes. It had an aura of the days of what was truly Western Music. I could almost imagine hearing old songs in the air, songs like "I've Got Spurs that Jingle Jangle Jingle," "Blue Shadows on the Trail," "Tumbling Tumbleweeds," "Cool Water," and other compositions having rhythm and chord structures that I refer to as the 1940s roll.

Walter Gant owned thousands of acres north of the lodge. These he intended to keep, but he wanted to get out from under the lodge and its liabilities. He wanted to sell the lodge, the motel unit, the house, and the stables to the east. He was offering these and eighty acres for $65,000. I made many pleas to some of my well-heeled friends to help me make the purchase and transform the place into an art institute, but none would. What a lost opportunity that was. I had a vision and no money. Some of my friends had money but no vision. The state of New Mexico purchased the lake from the Springer outfit, and then all the eighty acres became lakeside property adjacent to New Mexico's newest state park. Sadly, once we acquire financial abilities, oftentimes the opportunities are no longer there.

The marriage with Gilda crumbled, as did the lodge and the buildings around it, along with the opportunity to purchase it. Now, on very rare occasions, I drive the highway behind the place, the one that follows the Cimarron River down to the town of Cimarron and from there on to Springer. I stop the vehicle and muse. I look down upon the ruins, remembering both the good times and the bad times spent there, those times that were but fleeting seconds in the drama of life.

I remember hummingbirds by the dozens and Sawndra gasping in awe as one lit and perched upon her finger. I remember Cadmium Red, our Irish setter, and how she loved the mountains and streams. I remember her wearing a baseball cap upon her head and sunglasses over her eyes, placed on her by the kids as we drove around the area.

I remember sneaking down to the lake with Billy, trespassing upon the Springers, and catching moonlight trout. I remember the almost daily mountain thunderstorms, the rainbows, and the great majesty of the New Mexico landscape. I remember the trips into Red River, Questa, the Rio Grande River, and Taos. I remember the smells of pine trees, piñon burning in the fireplace, and coffee on frosty mornings.

I remember there was another old house down by the stables, long abandoned. No one lived there and had not lived there for decades. There was no electric power to the place, but now and then on dark nights, a light would appear in the windows, linger for a while, and then disappear. I did not one time go down to investigate.

I remember coming back, way past sundown, from the wild lower Red River where we had been trout fishing to find a note on the front door of the lodge left there by one of the managers of the Springer Land and Cattle Company. The note informed us that Cecil Gant

THE OLD HOUSE AND STABLES WHERE THE MYSTERIOUS LIGHT SHONE.

had gone to the hospital in Santa Fe, and there he had died. We were numbed with disbelief. Gilda's uncle had died!

We went into the lodge to get out of the chill, out of the dark, and to ponder what we should do. Cecil's body was in Santa Fe; we were at Eagle Nest; we had to leave the following morning to get the kids back to school in Sweeny, Texas, 800 miles distant from the lodge. I went back out to the VW Van to unload some items and looked at Cecil's house. I was dumbfounded by what I saw and hastily brought Gilda outside. "Look!" I said as I pointed to the structure. She gasped. That light, the one that Cecil always kept burning both day and night, had burned out!

XLI.
DIVINING

"WATER WITCHING" it is called by some. "Divining" it is called by others. Witchcraft, sorcerer's work, something occult, some proclaim. Some say it is a gift. Some say it is "the work of the Devil." Some scoff at it. Others swear by it. As for me, I do not believe in it, but I do not disbelieve in it, either. My artist friend Jim Eppler can spot a snake's head that is sticking out from under a rock at eighty yards in the distance when I cannot see it at all unless I use binoculars. How am I to know what some can perceive that I cannot perceive? I just may not have the ability to see or feel or sense some things that someone else can. Some people can dance, yet I have witnessed some who simply cannot begin to feel any rhythm at all, or if they do, they cannot translate it into kinetic movement that stays on beat.

After my purchase of the property that is now New Art, it came about that I needed a well. I bought eight acres on the Llano River in Mason County, Texas. There is a lot of water in the river, but I needed potable water. I needed well water. I needed water to hook up to the house and the studio that I was building. Where to drill became a major question. One does not just poke a hole in the ground and always "hit water" as it is termed. There are numerous dry holes in this area, especially on the north side of the Llano River. Back in the days of the early 1980s, the cost of drilling was twelve dollars per foot. These days, it is usually more than that, but with the current recession some drillers offer ten-dollar-a-foot drilling. One driller advertises five dollars per foot, but the word is out that he charges twelve dollars for the casing! It was unlikely that a well here would be less than one hundred feet in depth, and in those days $1,200 was a lot of money for me to spend. In those days I was a college art teacher. I had car payments. I paid rent in Houston, the city where I was then teaching. I had land payments. I had taxes to pay. I had the other expenses that people incur.

So it came to pass that I learned about Mayfield Kothmann, who claimed to be a water witcher. Kothmann is about as German a name as there is, but even so, Mayfield considered himself to be an American Indian. He had a vast collection of flint artifacts, many having been picked up on his property not far to the east of mine on the south side of the Llano River. Mayfield knew little about archaeology, even though the local gentry regarded him as an authority, and some even seemed to think he was an Indian. I think what he regarded as "tomahawk heads" were in fact large oval blades. These were likely knapped at least three thousand years ago. I think Mayfield might have thought they were fashioned into weapons used to war against White settlers. If that is actually what he thought, he was probably wrong.

Someone around Mason told me that Mayfield was a water witcher. I invested fifty dollars for his water witching services—even though I did not believe in water witching. It was quite interesting, though, watching him work. He would walk about the property holding his two brass rods in front of his chest, waiting for them to give him the proper sign. These were one-eighth inch brass brazing rods that were bent at right angles about eight inches from each rod's end.

As Mayfield walked about doing his witching, his elbows were bent almost up to his chest, and the rods were held in a manner so that the short ends were in his hands and the long ends were parallel to the earth and to each other and were protruding away from his body. He walked around and around, around and about, until the rods crossed. He said he could not hold them tightly enough to keep them from crossing. Then he walked away from the spot where they had crossed, and the rods went back to a parallel position. He walked back to where they had first crossed, and they crossed again. He did this several times and then marked an exact spot with a stone. "You have water here," he stated. "Now I will tell you how much you have."

He cut a small green twig from a box elder tree and carefully trimmed it with his pocketknife. He sat cross-legged, and with both hands he held the twig over the stone. It began bobbing, then stopped. He had counted the bobs. He stood. "You have fourteen gallons a minute here," he told me. "Now I will find out how deep it is."

Again he sat, and in the same position. The twig began bobbing, and he began counting. I was not counting the bobs, but Mayfield was. I was just beholding what he was doing while secretly being skeptical.

"You have three pays. You have water at thirty-five feet, fifty-five feet, and you have water at ninety feet." I wrote Mayfield a check for fifty dollars and marked the spot with a stone cairn. A year or so later, I contracted McGill Well Drilling Company in Eden, Texas, to come drill a well. We drilled precisely in that spot.

"Beats throwing a rock and drilling where it lands," the driller told me. He carefully logged the process. He hit water at thirty-five feet. He hit water at fifty-five feet. He hit another pay at ninety feet. We drilled to 120 feet in order to have 30 feet as a reserve column. There was water where Mayfield said there was water. But Mayfield was wrong! The well came in at fifteen gallons a minute, not fourteen gallons a minute!

On the property to my north, two dry holes were recently drilled. The most recent owner of this place does not believe in witching either, but he thought he might as well invest some money and have a witcher from London (Texas) come over and witch it. Mayfield died some twenty years ago. The London witcher charged $175. Inflation even hits the water witching business. The well came in at four and one-half gallons a minute. That is a good find on that property, although two and a half miles west, there is a well that produces 250 gallons a minute.

I know another witcher. He can witch caves, water pipes, electrical lines, and for certain—he avows—he can witch water. My friend Joel Locke has a place down river from me about four miles. His well went dry. Our mutual friend witched it for him. It was a dry hole. Our friend witched it again assuring him there is water below. Again, it was a dry hole. Our friend swears there is water there and that the driller just did not go deep enough. I have this question: if there is water there, and the driller just did not drill deep enough, why did they drill a second well about the same depth as the first hole instead of drilling half, or two times as deep again in the first dry hole?

Men will dig for gold, silver, and all sorts of treasures and never find any of them, but they will go to their graves thinking and believing if they had just dug one foot deeper...Now how are we going to counter that argument? Since no one dug "one foot deeper," how are we to know there was not a payload there? And again, who knows or who can know what mysterious, psychic powers of energy lie within some human's mind and within the chambers of his heart? And who can truly explain places of mystery, power and energy?

EPILOGUE

NO ONE CAN PROVE THE EXISTENCE of anything, perhaps. Maybe. Philosophers have argued this for centuries. Supposedly Rene Descartes stated, *"cogito ergo sum,"* meaning, "I think, therefore I am." So, should it be, "I think I saw and perceived these things, therefore they are?"

All our five—or six—senses sometimes may deceive us. They may do so in a manner similar to what is still indelible in my mind—a *Tyrannosaurus Rex* that I saw peep through the window of my parents house when I was eight years of age. My steel-trap brain still sees it. My logical mind tells me it could not have been.

I have changed some names in these writings. This, of course, is to avoid incurring someone's anger or perhaps embarrassing or humiliating someone. I did not change some of the names because I saw no reason to do so, and I chose not to do so in order to keep their memories alive. All of these stories are from my personal experiences, other than the Capote Falls episode, the Boyd Elder Valentine light episode, and one of the Marfa Lights episodes. These I have related as they were told to me, as best I can remember them, and I have no doubts about their credibility. What I have written here from my personal recollections and from my personal experiences is as much the truth as is *cogito ergo sum*. At the very least, it is the truth as I perceived it to be. One thing is certain—it is true these are my personal stories of mystery, power and energy. *Caveat lector!*

BILL WORRELL,
New Art, Texas

RIGHT: HER ROYAL BLACKNESS,
ELLIE MAY LUCILLE WORRELL.

A PARTING NOTE

I THINK FORGIVENESS IS AN ESSENTIAL TOOL of survival.

Take great care not to mistakenly perceive others to possess energies they do not have and will not have. Be cautious and do not blindly follow them.

Go to great lengths to avoid anyone who mistreats children or animals.

Go to great lengths to avoid anyone who mistreats anyone, or anything, including Planet Earth.

When Merle Haggard was inducted into the Country Music Hall of Fame, he let a ten-foot long scroll unfurl to the floor and said, "There is a long list of people I would like to thank. I would like to thank my plumber in Burbank..."

That is how I am now. Many souls have graced my life from the time of kindergarten to this moment: family, friends, enemies, teachers, galleries, collectors, and on and on and on. Due to a lack of space I could only begin (somewhat feebly) to make a complete list. Please know how grateful I am to each and every one of you.

WORRELL

Among those to whom I am most grateful is Ellie May Lucille Worrell
Carpe EVERY Diem

RIGHT: PEOPLE DUMP THE STRANGEST
THINGS. MIGHT AS WELL TAKE ADVANTAGE.

BIOGRAPHY

BILL WORRELL'S ART CAREER spans more than forty years. He holds a Bachelor of Arts degree in sociology with a minor in English and teaching certification in art education from Texas Tech University. He was awarded a Master of Fine Arts degree in painting and drawing with a minor in sculpture from the University of North Texas, where he also held a doctoral fellowship. He was Associate Professor of Art at Odessa College, and was Professor of Art at Houston Baptist University. He has served on the advisory board of UNT School of Art and Visual design.

Worrell left the classroom in 1989 to devote full time to his artistic pursuits and to become a "recovering teacher." (He acknowledges that he is recovering more from legislation than from teaching.) His sculptures, paintings, and jewelry are in fine art galleries across the country, and his works are in collections around the world.

Worrell is a person of wide and varied interests. He has appeared on the NBC Today Show, The Nashville Network, and in music videos with Brooks and Dunn and other Nashville personalities. In 1996 the Odessa Heritage Foundation named Worrell as one of the city's outstanding former citizens. The University of North Texas named him as an outstanding graduate in 2009. In 2009 Colorado High School honored Worrell by naming him an outstanding graduate of that school. He has been featured in Southwest Art Magazine and other publications, and he has also been featured on the Texas Country Reporter and the Sounds of Texas. Gold medal awards have been earned for wine labels he designed.

Bill Worrell is an outdoors man, inventor, philosopher, songwriter, music-maker, and lover of life. His three published books are *Voices from the Cave – the Shamans Speak, Colorado City, Texas* and *Journeys Through The Winds of Time*. He currently has five other books in progress. Highway 29 Records published his CD, *Carpe **EVERY** Diem* in 2006. Other musical works have been published by Boosey & Hawks and performed at Carnegie Hall, Spivey Hall, and at the National Association of Chorale Directors Meeting in Vancouver.

The oldest pictorial art in North America is in Texas, on the Lower Pecos River and the Middle Rio Grande. For the past three decades Worrell's paintings and sculptures have helped make this area known around the world. His monumental sculpture, "The Maker of Peace," graces the entrance to the Texas Seminole Canyon Historical State Park. This park is located on a tributary of the Rio Grande a few miles east of Lantry, Texas, home of the infamous Judge Roy Bean. Seminole Canyon derives it's name not from the Ancient Texans who created the pictographs, but for the Seminole Indians who were scouts for the U.S. Calvary in the 1800's.

Bill Worrell and Ellie May Lucille, a wonderful Golden-doodle, reside beside the Llano River in Mason County, near Art, Texas. They also reside part time in Santa Fe, New Mexico, and in a Ford Expedition on the beautiful highways of the Southwest.

CPSIA information can be obtained at www.ICGtesting.com
Printed in the USA
LVOW01s1915311013

359239LV00004B/8/P